What C
Saying About
GET UP!

"This book is a testimony of strength, courage and faith. Rodney encourages you to think positive, never give up and keep working hard towards your dreams. His ability to surpass obstacles, overcome adversity, and rise to his level of success is truly amazing. For all he has done and continues to do to help those around him speaks volumes about his heart! Rodney Flowers is truly an inspiration."
—Peggy McColl, New York Times Bestselling author

"Rodney Flowers is a man who has shown determination, tenacity, and an unwillingness to give up when most of us would have. In spite of the hardship he endured, he did not give up and has not only helped himself but is helping others along his courageous and successful journey. This book is a must read for anybody interested in succeeding in life and rising above near-impossible circumstances."

—Judy O'Beirn, creator & co-author of International bestselling book *Unwavering Strength*

"When we know something personal about the author of a book, we read their words through the lens of that perception. Try this one on for size: A fifteen year old boy suddenly paralyzed from the neck down. That changes everything and every word that Rodney Flowers speaks to you in "Get Up." Indeed, knowing the remarkable truth of his story gives deep meaning to every sentence, because he's the epitome of the difference between 'talking the talk' and 'walking the walk'. His heartfelt,

motivating message will take up private residence within, and provide an empowerment you can make use of . . . every day. Read on and be blessed. "

—**Little John Behan,** The Ambassador of Gratitude

"I absolutely love this book. It is moving and inspiring in a way that I haven't seen in a long time. The solid and detailed advice is simple and clear to understand (but not easy). This book has my highest recommendation. If you want higher success, buy it now!"

—**Stephen Whiteley,** Inspirational Man of the Year and author of the award winning book *"Happiness Works! Get Yours Here!*

"Get Up! . . . is one of the best 'how-to' riveting true stories proving, with authentic principles, the idea that your mind is your greatest asset. Rodney Flowers knows YOU CAN because HE DID! His message is crystal clear for anyone needing a 'leg up' to go another inch. With deep certainty and wisdom, he declares "Don't Just Do it for You; Do it for Those that Need to See You Do it." We all know inside that nothing says 'YOU CAN' like someone who did! You will see yourself clearly in the 'will and spirit' of Rodney Flowers. This book is a movie waiting to happen."
—**Anya Sophia Mann,** International Bestselling Author, Visionary Intuitive Consultant

"What do you do when you get knocked down from the pinnacle of life? How do you recover when you find yourself stuck in the darkest place imaginable, unable to move? You have one of two choices: You languish in the quagmire or . . . you GET UP! Rodney Flowers did just that. He got up. From the insightful words you are about to read, he shares with us his unique, yet beautiful journey navigating this horrific storm in his life. As it is written in the Kabbalah, the ancient mystical text

of Judaism: "It is the falls of our life that provide us the energy to be propelled to a higher level." Rodney has transcended a life-changing injury by accepting it as a gift from God. From it he has learned much about himself and about life. He has grown immensely and now stands tall. GET UP! I Can't. I Will. I Did . . . Here's How is a must read."
—**Dr. Terry A. Gordon,** author of *No Storm Lasts Forever;* American Heart Association National Physician of the Year 2002

"This amazing book will inspire you to persevere with the same grit and faith he used to get up out of what restrictions spoke over him. This will inspire you to use the same grit to overcome your personal obstacles. Thank you Rodney for inspiring me."
—**Willie Tart,** Bestselling Co-Author, *Unwavering Strength Volume 1*

"Get Up, I Can't, I Will, I Did... Here's How .... Is a perfect title for Rodney Flowers new book. Rodney provides a clear message in this book that whatever challenge life has seen fit to give you there is a reason, a purpose and plan to overcome it. It is abundantly clear that Rodney recognized a divine purpose for his life and that along with his personal "grit" he paved a path that defied the odds. Rodney learned how to listen past the doctors and tune into his own channel and in doing so found his true path and purpose which he has so eloquently shared so others can follow. Get Up is an inspirational journey of empowerment and the story of a young man who became a man beyond his dreams."

—**Janet Love,** Author Lyme Empowerment: *A Road Map to the Origins of Health*

GET UP!

I Can't. I Will. I Did.

Here's How . . .

RODNEY C. FLOWERS

Permission should be addressed in writing to:
Rodney Flowers, PO Box 1308, Leonardtown, MD 20650 or
Rodney@RodneyFlowers. Com

Editor, Justin Spizman

Cover Design, Killer Covers
www. KillerCovers. Com

Layout, DocUmeant Designs
www. DocUmeantDesigns. Com

First Edition, 2015

ISBN-13: 978-0-9920116-1-1
ISBN-10: 0992011612

CONTENTS

ACKNOWLEDGEMENTS

Elizabeth Carol Sinclair:

To my Mother: I can only imagine the pain and agony you felt while watching your only son experience such a tragic accident, and then struggle profusely to regain his strength, ability, and dignity. I am not only proud, but also grateful to say I have a mother like you constantly looking out for me, protecting my best interests and offering so much compassion and conviction. Most of all, I am appreciative of your faith, trust, and belief in me and the power of God. You never gave up on me and no matter how difficult it was, you always-always-always pushed me beyond my normal limits. There's no way I could ever repay you for the strength, determination, and outright will you have instilled in me. My aggression for life is a direct reflection of you and for that I say thank you for all you have done. May this book provide consolation to your efforts, your faith, and your know-how to win.

I love you dearly and forever I always will. . . .

James Louis Sinclair:

To my Father: This journey has been a combination of bumps and bruises from the very beginning. Who knew things would turn out the way they did. I am a better man thanks to you. Your smooth approach towards life and humble confidence has provided me with a gateway to success. Thank you for providing your view and perspective towards the obstacles and challenges we all face. Your patience and understanding, as well as your outlook on life, were like a breath of fresh air. You always had just the right words to say to help me make it through another day. I am in debt to your commitment, loyalty, and counseling. Your fatherhood has been unprecedented.

My love for you will never cease.

Marquita Evette Hill:

To my Sister: I could not have been blessed with a more compassionate, trustworthy, loving, and considerate sister as you. You have been my best friend, a smiling face, and a person who eloquently put me back in my place when I was out of line. I've watched you grow from a little girl to an amazing woman. I must say that I am proud of the woman you have become and the family you created. Without you, my life would probably have turned out much different. You are an integral part of my success. During the difficult times in my life, our friendship was often all that I had to look forward to. You kept me going when everything within me wanted to stop. Your maturity and your playfulness provided hope in a time of darkness. Thank you for all you've done and for whom you have become. I love you.

You truly are the greatest little sister, a big brother could have.

Mr. and Mrs. Betty and William Breeden:

To my best friends: You all have been the true definition of friends to my family and I. Your presence will always be welcomed. You have a way of providing lightness in a heavy situation. I will always consider you both family as there's just no other way of viewing it. In our most desperate time of need, you guys were there to support us through thick and thin. I will never forget you and what you all have done. You have left a mark and an impression upon my family and I that will last forever. I can only hope that you are as proud of me as I am proud to have friends and family like you.

With love from me to you. Thank you for all that you are. . . .

Dr. Syvalla Washington, and the Cromartie Temple of Praise:

To my Church: Words cannot express the gratitude and appreciation that I have for the Cromartie Temple of Praise and its Spiritual Leader, Dr. Washington. You have truly been a guiding light, a church on which I could lean. You have held me up when I could not hold myself, you lifted me when I could not lift myself, and you danced for me when I could no longer dance on my own. At one point, your faith and belief that I could do the impossible was all the faith that I had. You lit the fire that now burns with a blaze in my soul. Your love and praise has provided a pathway to a source of possibilities. You truly are a righteous people and your prayers have been answered. I am proud to be a member of a church family that serves its people wholeheartedly. Thank you for your love and your prayers. I will always call your place of worship my home.

I love you all with all my heart.

Pearl Rhone and Neil Oxendine:

To my Therapists: You all have to be the greatest Physical and Occupational Therapist on the planet. A Dynamic Duo. We have come a long way since the first time we met. I am thankful that your support resonated from day one, and you were always willing to allow me to dream big. Although my chances of recovery was slim to none, you both stepped up and helped to get me out of my wheelchair and into a place of independence. Most noteworthy was your focus and efforts toward helping me walk across the stage and receive my diploma at my high school graduation. Thank you for believing in me and assisting me in accomplishing this major task. It was a pivotal moment for me and set the tone as the first of many major accomplishments during my road to recovery. You will never be forgotten, and can never be replaced as the greatest Physical and Occupational Therapists on the planet.

May God bless you and your families will love and warmth.

Joyce Ann Floyd:

To my Friend: I miss you in a very special way. You always brought a smile upon my face. Like a big sister I never had, you had kind words and a way of picking me up when I was down. I still remember the days you would load me up in my full-size van and drive me around town to show me a good time. You were there for me and my only regret is that I didn't get a chance to thank you enough. I appreciate what you've done for me. I could count on you to support me in any and everything that I wanted to do. In many ways you made things happen for me. You and your family are my family. I love you and miss you beyond words.

May your spirit be with us forever and always. . . .

Sherona Rolynn Thomas:

To my Angel: You have been my Spring, a new beginning, and a gift that keeps on giving. You are joy in the midst of trouble and sunshine creeping over the horizon. Your smile brightens my day. Your friendship has been invaluable and your care for me has been unmatched. I am grateful for you and all that we share. The journey that we've traveled has been pleasant and pleasing. I respect and appreciate you for all that you've done, for all that you do, and for the person you are. You have been there for me. Your presence has been essential.

Thank you for being you. I will love you always. . . .

Remaining family and friends:

To everyone else: With 10,000 tongues I could not express how grateful I am for the support, guidance, encouragement, and inspiration you have given me. I am blessed to be encased around such wonderful, beautiful people whom have poured out their hearts for the greater good. I am humbled by your compassion. In return, my desire is to make you all proud. Hopefully this book accomplishes that, for it was all of you whom I thought about as I wrote these pages. Not only have you compelled me to press forward, reach for my goals, and break the chains of my wheelchair, but you have compelled me to go even farther. To not only fly, but to soar. Soar as the eagles soar with the wind beneath my wings. Without the support that you have given me, I would never have reached the goals I set.

Much love to you. May God be with you now and always.

NAVAIR Systems Command:

To AIR-2.0: One of the most beneficial lessons life can teach is the value of life itself. All too often this lesson is learned the hard way; some unforeseen circumstances raises our level of consciousness of just how short but precious life can be. As a result of it all, we gain a higher understanding that nothing should be taken for granted. I am grateful for the opportunity to serve the mission of such a wonderful organization. You have proven to be the organization of choice for equal employment opportunities. The accommodations as well as the training and leadership opportunities you provided are exceptional. As a result of my personal experience, this is the organization I recommend to individuals, disabled and able-bodied alike, seeking career development, advancement, and training, as well as individual growth.

Thank you . . . Sincerely

FOREWORD

Rodney suffered a terrible accident at the age of 15. His doctors told him he would never walk again. Yet, when I met him at one of my seminars some 20 years later, Rodney was walking.

Rodney was an incredible inspiration to everyone in the room that day. He is such an extraordinary guy that when he told me he was writing a book, I told him to send it to me. And he did.

As I read *Get Up!*, I was even more inspired by his story. I've worked with thousands of people who were striving to make a dream come true, but few, if any, had to face and overcome such a devastating blow. You see, Rodney had his heart set on making it to the National Football League, and he was working very hard toward that dream. Then, in a flash, his dream was ripped away and he was bound to the confines of a wheelchair.

Many people would have given up after receiving such a dire prognosis. But Rodney didn't listen to people who told him why something couldn't be done. He absolutely refused to let anything that was going on outside stop him. Instead of feeling sorry for himself, Rodney learned to control how he thinks feels, and acts. And that made all the difference in the world.

There are many gems to reap from Rodney's story, but one thing really sticks out for me. He turned a nightmare into a dream by learning to live in harmony with the principles of success. Everyone who wins must do that—whether they do it consciously or unconsciously.

Rodney's life demonstrates that it's what we think that ultimately manifests into results. Through faith, belief and focus he was able to overcome the odds to not only walk again, but to make a positive impact on the world.

This book is an excellent investment. It is rich with valuable strategies to show you the steps you must take if you want to joyfully live with purpose and realize your dreams. As you move through each chapter, you might be surprised by Rodney's candor. He has chosen to share many of the terrifying experiences from his accident and prognosis with you. The lessons he has learned and gleaned from each experience will inspire you.

George Bernard Shaw once said, *"People are always blaming their circumstances for what they are. I don't believe in circumstances. The people who get on in this world are the people who get up and look for the circumstances they want, and if they can't find them, make them."*

Rodney is one of those people. He is a real-life example of getting up and getting on even in the face of horrific circumstances. This book will make you realize that you can conquer just about anything. That's not an exaggeration and it's not a fairy tale. It's real.

Bob Proctor

INTRODUCTION

As a very determined individual, I began spring training earlier than most. For the 1993 football season, my training started during the first month of the year, well before most of my team-mates would even consider running their first laps or doing their first set of push-ups. I knew if I wanted to be above the average high school football player, I'd have to get started earlier than the average high school football player. My dream was to go Pro. I knew that there were millions of other high schools players with that same dream, and realized that only the ones who worked the hardest, had the biggest heart, made the most sacrifices, and most importantly, had the greatest love for the game of football would be part of the few that lived out their dream. My mind was made up, and my heart was set for the National Football League. My goal was to perform like a collegiate player in high school, like a professional player once I was in college, and like a veteran professional player once I made it to the Pros. I had it all planned out. The love for the game, along with this frame of thinking acted as my backbone and foundation to reach my goals. With this strategy in mind, I dedicated my entire life and body to the game of football.

However, life had other plans for me. Plans for a bigger dream. A better dream. One that would inspire, motivate, and even help others. Ironically enough, this dream started as a nightmare. It was hor-rific in every way. My dream started with a moment of pure horror. You see, in a split second, I lost my ability to walk. I was paralyzed in a freak accident on the football field. I trained so hard. I longed for the opportunity. However I was given something entirely different. As a young boy in high school, I shifted from a career in football to the hope of walking again. My hopes and aspirations of playing in the pros was quickly replaced with hopes and aspirations of per-forming the simplest things in life like walking and independently performing the activities of daily living such as bathing, dressing and taking care of myself. With nowhere to turn, and no answer to the solution, I had to turn inward and find the faith, strength, and mental know-how to refrain from dying an emotional death. I had to get up from the unexpected blow that life dished out. As a result of this horror, I developed a new dream.

Walking again became my dream. If only I could put one foot in front of the other. Eventually I did. And it is this book that takes you on that journey. Not only will you experience all of the challenges of spinal trauma, but you will also receive the tools and principles that propelled victory and success into my life. These principles are proven, tried and tested. Real-life lessons learned as a result of determination and a will to get up and win the game of life even in the face of ridiculous odds.

There's no greater example than a real-life example. One that we all can live by. This book provides just that. My life is a real-life example that will inspire, motivate, and encourage you to get up and conquer your dreams, no matter how big or small. Whatever challenges you face today can be conquered tomorrow.

In life, we all experience setbacks, challenges, and obstacles. We all have goals that we would like to achieve. And at times, we all need a little nudge or push to get us over the edge. No matter where you are in life, this book will give you the guidance to get up and go to a higher level. Whether you've hit rock bottom and just looking for a way out, or on the brink of conquering your ultimate goal, this book will give you what you need to get up and get it done. You're about to embark on a journey that will bring about change. A transformation! A transformation that will bring about success and lead to greatness.

Climb 'Til Your Dream Comes True

Often your tasks will be many,

And more than you think you can do.

Often the road will be rugged

And the hills insurmountable, too.

But always remember, the hills ahead

Are never as steep as they seem,

And with Faith in your heart start upward

And climb 'Til you reach your dream.

For nothing in life that is worthy

Is never too hard to achieve

If you have the courage to try it

And you have the Faith to believe.

For Faith is a force that is greater

Than knowledge or power or skill

And many defeats turn to triumph

If you trust in God's wisdom and will.

For Faith is a mover of mountains.

There's nothing that God cannot do,

So start out today with Faith in your heart

And "Climb 'Til Your Dream Comes True"!

~ Helen Steiner Rice (1900 - 1981)

(*Helen Steiner Rice Poems: Inspirational and Friendship Poems,* 2014)

Chapter 1

GRIT UP RATHER THAN GIVE UP

We have all heard the term grit. It is a quality, a characteristic of sorts, that stands for a never give-up mentality. It thrives on your ability to dig in, with a refusal to fail attitude. Grit is what separates those that fall short from those that get up when they fall short. It is a hard and fast way to determine how far you will go in life, and how much you can overcome on your journey.

As the first Chapter in our voyage together, Grit Up Rather than Give Up is of fundamental importance. You may certainly possess the necessary skills to win, you may have what it takes to accomplish amazing things in life, but you'll never reach your goals if you give up before you get there. You'll never know what it feels like to win. Grit Up Rather than Give Up is deciding to win the game of life, regardless of how much effort is required, instead of allowing life to simply defeat you. It means that you ignite your life with fire and a determined attitude, and demand from yourself the effort necessary to reach your goals or overcome any situation. It's standing in the face of challenge and adversity with the mindset to win.

Grit is not just ordinary determination, but gut-busting and driven determination that can't be tamed, nor stopped. Grit Up Rather than Give Up means fighting until the very last breath and exhausting all possibilities before you stop. It means not taking no for an answer. Not believing in the word can't, and finding a way, some-how, deep within yourself, to make it happen regardless of the odds, or chance for failure.

Grit means not settling for what life has thrown at you, but rather, throwing back punches of determination and will to accomplish, to win, and to be whatever it is that you desire to be. It means search-ing deep within yourself and identifying your fabric and DNA that resides within. Grit is reaching so deep inside yourself that you lit-erally turn yourself inside out, redefining who you are in order to be what you desire.

At the age of 15, I was paralyzed from the neck down from a freak football accident. Upon suffering a C5/C6 spinal cord injury, the doctors determined that I would have to learn how to live with this difficult diagnosis, and they then outlined the necessary equipment that I would need in order to live a normal life.

Normal? Not a chance. The first significant change I made was in how I moved from point A to point B. My electronic wheelchair would be my new home. Home health care and vehicle modifica-tions were the hot dinner topics for us. We didn't know how to deal with an injury like this. Life was turned upside down. But there was no cure for spinal cord trauma and my condition was not going away. There was nothing anyone could do for me. There was only the hope that my body would heal itself, or that God would per-form a miracle. Frankly, I wasn't sure of either. The only options available were to either accept my condition and lose at the game of life, or fight like hell and try to relocate some sense of normalcy.

I knew the odds were against me to overcome this injury. I knew that most paralyzed people remain so for the rest of their lives. I knew that I could exert an enormous amount of effort and still never walk again. In fact, doctors told me it was very unlikely I would walk again.

At that point, I had every right to give up and give in, and I felt like doing so . . . My medical practitioners and experts would provide hope in the form of testimonials from other paralyzed people who lived productive and happy lives with their conditions. However, I could not mentally grasp that concept. I could not see myself in a wheelchair for the rest of my life. The thought of that made me sick to my stomach. It brought about pain to my emotions and my mind. I simply could not live with the notion that I would forever be destined to reside in a wheeled chair. That just didn't work for me.

Something had to change. Something had to happen. I wasn't about to accept this situation. And at that moment I made a decision that I was going to change my current condition or die trying. A switch in my mind flipped and I decided I would overcome paralysis and learn how to walk again. I was comfortable with either result. That meant it didn't matter how long it was going to take or how hard it was going to be. I was willing to try as hard as I could, even to the point of death. And I was willing to try as long as I could, even if it meant all of my earthly life. Although my family and some of my friends were there to support me, it still felt like I was at it alone.

At only 15 years of age, I didn't know how to handle that type of mental stress. There was no class for it. It is definitely not taught in school. No one could tell me how to feel or how not to feel. All I felt was pain. Excruciating pain. Just knowing I was paralyzed was devastating. Unfortunately, the only person that could end it was me; and the odds weren't in my favor.

Ever since I suffered this traumatic incident, I've had to reach and pull beyond measure in an effort to regain and recover my physical ability. I had to grit up. Doctors told me I would never walk again and that I would be paralyzed from the neck down till the day I died. I could have easily gave up and settled for the advice of medical experts. Life in a wheelchair, paralyzed from the neck down for the rest of my life. But I did not. I mentally and physically defeated the odds of being in a wheelchair for the rest of my life.

For me, grit is an unstoppable, unmovable, and unshakable determination. It is sustained effort and resolve that outweighs and outlasts the longevity of every obstacle placed in the way of your destination. It is unbreakable faith in one's ability to accomplish a desired outcome and is the attitude of winning by any ethical or morally acceptable means necessary. It is the compilation of courage, determination, faith, and extreme endurance to outlast, fight through, push around, or run over any and everything that gets in the way of your accomplishments or desired goals. It is doing whatever it takes, for however long it takes, no matter what it takes. It is overcoming the feeling of laziness, tiredness, and all physical and mental limitations and pushing beyond what is socially expected to a realm of possibilities currently unknown to you.

I have to dig deep to secure enormous grit on a daily basis. For years on end, I was tasked to relearn many of the basic functions of my life. Standing up, moving my feet, walking, controlling my body, and eventually, shedding the wheelchair. It took more grit and dedication than I ever imagined. I knew the journey would be long and difficult, but it surpassed even my boldest expectations. You know you are in for one heck of a battle when your team of physicians constantly starts their statements to you with, "Rodney, it is unlikely you will ever . . . " Being on the receiving end of that declaration was not only horrifying, but also completely debilitating. If nothing else, you always have hope. But hope begins to subside when reality sets in. The only way I found I could regain that valuable currency of hope was through declaring, on a daily basis, that I would have substantial amounts of grit.

My personal view of grit is giving it everything that you have. It is nonstop effort fueled by the unwavering desire to a reach a goal. It is reaching deep within your soul, within your very being and finding ability beyond what is currently known to you. Grit is continuing to press forward when everything around you says it's not worth it. It is making a way out of no way. It is reaching beyond your current predicament into the sea of possibility. Grit is understanding and knowing that you can do the impossible. It is the singular act of believing that you have what it takes. It is the difference between great and legendary. It is the attitude of I will. It is the strength of 100,000 men focused on one goal, and on one purpose. It is the

Rocky Balboa of effort. It is a mountain of determination. It is an ocean of will. It is the Niagara Falls of faith. It is the Grand Canyon of endurance.

Grit is a characteristic and quality close to my heart. Looking back at my journey, I humbly recognize the many different occasions when I had no choice but to make a decision between gritting up or giving up. In hindsight, it was not always an easy decision. Giving up was the comfortable play. It was much easier. But somehow, someway, I always dug deep and located the grit I needed to survive. In the beginning, all I focused on was surviving each day. Grit really matters when your victories are small and few and far in between. So to take a lesson from my life and implement it into yours, our journey together begins by waking up each and every day of your life and agreeing to never give up, and always find the grit you need to overcome, overachieve, and over-succeed.

Chapter 2

FAILURE: NOT AN OPTION

G rit Up Rather than Give Up is based on the notion that you always have just a little more sweat equity to give to your goals. Your heart and soul always offer you the opportunity to find just a few more ounces of fuel to drive you forward. Grit goes hand in hand with the notion that failure is simply not an option. If you subscribe to this motto, you will probably agree that grit helps to ensure you are fail proof. Now, sometimes you may fall short of your goals. But it's not failure if you gave all you had and are left with nothing in the grit tank.

Within my own life, I subscribe to the notion that success is not an outcome but rather it is a journey. It is the culmination of all I gave to the process. Failure: Not an Option means that I cannot, shall not, and will not be defeated. There's no possible way I will allow myself to lose. However, instead I will ensure that I will win by developing strategies, routines, and habits that will increase my skills, enhance my character, and peak my performance in order to succeed.

In 1993, it was the third day of my sophomore year. I played high school football for the Lumberton Pirates. It was our very first game of the season, and we were playing the South View Tigers on our home field. I lined up on the right side of the field as we prepared for the kick-off to the second half of the game. As the placekicker made contact with the ball, I ran down the field while remaining mindful to stay in my lane and avoid other players. As I approached my opponent's forty-yard line, I saw the Tiger's kick returner heading towards my side of the field. In preparation to tackle the other team's player, I made a slight left turn in his direction. Traveling at top speed, I broke into tackling form and made contact with the South View Tiger's kick returner. I remember the hit as a fierce one. I felt the runner go down. I too went down, but after hitting the ground, something didn't seem right. Upon contact, it felt as if all of my energy and power jumped out of my body. I couldn't feel myself. I tried to get up. I knew what it felt like to get up. My brain was repeatedly going through the process of getting up, but my body was unresponsive. It became clear I was unable to move and would not be getting up on my own. I immediately knew I was in bad shape. I kept trying to get up. I heard people shouting, "Get up Rodney, get up." I knew I suffered some sort of spinal injury.

My teammate and best friend ran to me after the hit and said forcefully, "Good hit man. That's what I'm talking about, good hit." Then he realized something was wrong. He reached down to help. "Are you alright man? C'mon lets go, get up." But before he had a chance to grab my hands, the coaches and trainer stopped him and yelled, "Don't touch him, don't move him. He could be hurt badly." Reality began to set in and tears began to roll down my face. I came to grip with the fact that the only thing I had control over was my head. I could not feel or move my arms and legs.

I felt like I failed my team. I felt unfortunate and sorry that I couldn't get up. As I laid on the field looking into their faces, the coaches and trainers were panicked. I kept yelling out, "I can't move, I can't feel my legs. Somebody help me. Help me get up." The coaches attempted to calm me down. By then my mom had made her way to the field. As she knelt beside me she yelled, "Get up Rodney, get up." With tears running down her face, I responded, "I'm trying to get up. I'm trying. I can't." As she motioned to grab me and help me get up, the coaches pulled her away. Yelling frantically and fighting to get loose from them, she yelled, "That's my son, that's my baby." Gathering all the strength she could, she returned to my side only to find me even more frantic. With tears rolling down my face, I cried out, "help me! I can't move! I can't feel my legs. I can't move my body." Thoughts of never being able to walk began to creep into my mind and increase with every passing moment. I was so afraid. In that moment, I didn't have many options. All I could do was lay on that field, wondering if my life was over. But as the seconds turned into minutes, the minutes into hours, and the hours into days, I realized that failure could not be an option.

Failure has played a great role in my life. Not because I deem my life a failure, but rather, because I constantly flirted with the notion of failing. When you lose control of your bodily functions, you often have to consider that your life is a failure. However, I chose not to live that life. It took some time, but I eventually decided that I would make my life a success. Failure was never an experience I was willing to accept, and so, despite the challenge ahead of me, I decided I was going to win at the game of life. As you can imagine, after suffering paralysis, your mind fills with thoughts of inadequacy, fear, hopelessness, and defeat. You know you're going to have to fight back or you are sure to lose not only your physical ability, but also your sense of self-worth. Immediately you realize the gravity of the situation. Having lost my physical ability, I've had to sharpen my mind in order to give myself a fighting chance at winning and experiencing happiness in my life. I was dealing with a situation that could consume me both mentally and emotionally.

It didn't happen immediately, but in order to overcome what most would consider failure or defeat, I developed strategies, routines, plans, and habits that offered the greatest possibility to regain my physical ability, enhance my character, and peak my performance both physically and mentally. I demand more from myself than anyone and I developed the attitude that whatever it takes to regain my strength and ability would be exactly what I would dig down and give to the challenge ahead.

Upon my initial rehabilitation evaluation, my physical therapist wasn't sure how to evaluate me. I was willing to do anything if it would get me out of the wheelchair. However, a review of my medical records demonstrated little hope. The idea was to go through the initial evaluation and optimistically hope we'd see some signs of recovery. My physical therapy sessions involved lots and lots of stretching. To start, we spent all our time together stretching. The idea was to remain loose and flexible because spinal cord injuries have a tendency to cause a lot of rigidness within the muscles.

During the early stages of rehab, I vividly remember my physical therapist inquiring of my goals. I looked her straight in the eyes and told her that I wanted to walk again. I specifically told her that my goal was to walk out of this hospital. She looked back at me with a glare on her face that told me she did not think that was possible. But she did not want to upset me or offer the brutal truth. Hope has great healing powers. I had a determined look on my face and I wanted to show her that I was willing to stop at nothing in order to accomplish my goal. Failure was not an option. She asked me to move my legs, but I couldn't move them. She said, "Well we're going to have to get more out of you than that in order for you to walk again." I then lay on a mat and she put my legs and knees in a slightly bent position. She then asked me to straighten out my legs. Again, I could not do it. She asked me to try harder. Still, nothing.

Other physical therapists made the suggestion of trying electrical stimulation to jump-start the nerves and see if they would begin to work. So we did. My physical therapist placed electrodes on various locations of my skin in order to recruit the appropriate muscle fibers necessary to create a muscle contraction. Electrical stimulation uses an electrical current to cause a single muscle or group of muscles to contract.

The objective of contracting the muscles via electrical stimulation was to retrain my nervous system on the process of sending a signal from my brain to the stimulated area below the level of injury and vice versa. Once the electrical stimulation unit was turned on and created contractions, my job was to focus on contracting my muscles during the same time the electrical unit was contracting them. My therapist and I completed this process twice a day for several weeks. After each session, the electrodes were removed and the physical therapist motivated me to contract my muscles without her help. The first two weeks of the electrical stimulation training was very disappointing. It felt like a series of failure with no progress. I tried my hardest. I gave it my best. I strained and strained and strained to get my muscles to move. But the signals just weren't getting there. It wasn't until about three weeks of this training that I experienced a small contraction in my left thigh. This wasn't a real strong contraction. It was a very faint one. It seems as though only one muscle fiber in my entire quadriceps contracted. Out of all the straining and pushing and pulling, that one little faint muscle contraction was all I could come up with.

However, that was enough. My therapist and my entire rehabilitation team were elated by the fact that I was able to contract my quadriceps. They immediately called the doctor to have him take a look. It took everything I had in order to make the muscle contract again. But I was able to do so to allow the Doctor to see it. My Doctor seemed rather nonchalant about the whole ordeal. He was familiar with my injury, and based on his experience, he knew there was a slim chance I'd ever walk again. So he just suggested I continued to work hard and learn the necessary skills to be as independent as possible. Although disappointed by his reaction, I did not allow this to shake my faith. I continued to press hard in therapy, and execute all of the suggestions and recommendations made by my rehabilitation team. Whenever I felt negative emotions such as fear, hopelessness, discouragement, or defeat, I would try to replace those emotions with thoughts and actions that moved me towards my goal. Instead of feeling sorry for myself, I would think about and identify things I could be doing that would aid in my recovery. I made daily attempts towards blocking out all negative influences from my mind and only allowed positive influences to surround me. Whenever I experienced situations where I fell short of my desired outcome, I tried again and again and again until I overcame the shortfall and experienced the success I desired.

In every failure, there is an equal and opposite advantage of success. Failure is only a state of mind and in every failure, if you look close enough, there's something that you win or gain as a result of the failure. Failure should never be an option. It wasn't then for me, and it isn't now. Today, I walk without the help of a chair with wheels on it. But boy did it take a whole lot of small successes to get to that point. But even when I fell short, I never viewed it as a failure. I subscribed to the notion that I did not fail if I could look myself in the mirror and whole-heartedly declare I gave it my all. Sure, you may have fallen short. But falling short is not failing. Giving up is failing. Quitting is failing. Thus, the key here is to overcome each and every shortcoming along your journey toward success, even if it takes multiple attempts. Sure, you may pass through iterations of falling short and trying again and again. However, it doesn't really matter how many times it takes you to overcome your obstacles, or how long it may take. What matters most is that you overcome each and every shortfall that is preventing you from experiencing your destined success. I'm sure we agree that the path to success is not always easy, but failure is not ever an option. You'll probably find few people that wanted to give up and give in as much as I did. But it just wasn't in my fabric, and not part of my DNA. We, collectively and individually, can achieve great levels of success if we simply subscribe to the notion that failure is never an option.

Don't Just Do it for You; Do it for Those that Need to See You Do it

In life, we all need inspiration and the ability to look to others and feel the inner power that pushes us farther than we can go on our own. That inspiration may come from loved ones, those that have supported you along the way, or even from people you have never met. But rest assured, there are plenty of people that need to see you overcome your obstacles in life or reach that dream you've made your goal. There are plenty of people that need to see you do it not just for yourself, but for them as well. John Quincy Adams said, "If your actions inspire others to dream more, learn more, do more and become more, you are a leader."

As individuals, we all have a huge responsibility to do all we can to fulfill our purpose and/or dreams in life. You never know who's watching you. Your drive, determination, and will to succeed could act as someone else's motivation and inspiration. Reaching for your goals not only brings a great reward to you, but also rewards those associated with you. The fruits of your labor are ultimately the inspiration that pushes them towards their goals. Sometimes people need to see the success of those close to them to realize that they too can be successful. Your actions could be the outline, guide, and pathway leading to someone else's success. Tony Dorsett said, "To succeed, you need to find something to hold on to, something to motivate you, something to inspire to." Collectively, our goal is to be that inspiration for others. The reward for success is not just for you, but it is for those who come in contact with you, whether you know it or not.

I knew only one route during my battle back from paralysis. I had to succeed. I had to first do it for me, and then for everyone else. I never thought of my journey as an inspiration to others, but it is comforting to know it has played a role in helping friends and family overcome as well. I've learned that I've touched the lives of thousands of people I met along my journey. People whom I've never seen or talked to approached me and said that I have inspired, motivated, or made them feel like they can't complain about anything that life throws in their direction.

My daily attitude towards life triggers an emotion in them that makes them grateful and want to accomplish more for their own lives. Perhaps this trigger would have been activated in my absence or if I had not decided to get up and live successfully despite my injury. However, I am enormously grateful to be a cornerstone and a turning point towards the success for thousands of others. Remember when Ralph Waldo Emerson said, "Our chief want is someone who will inspire us to be what we know we could be." Frankly, I come from the school of thought that we are all dying to be inspired. It is a need, a want, and an endless journey to reach that exciting potential. Unfortunately, most of us lock our full potential away deep within the essence of our being and never to be discovered. This results in a loss to us all.

Sometimes in life we have a tendency to put others on a pedestal. We put them so far above ourselves that we don't think we can accomplish the things that they've accomplished. We use them as measuring sticks of which we can never measure. We believe they are simply more capable of extraordinary things while we simultaneously look at our lives as average or normal. But the reality is that we are all capable of reaching an enormous level of success.

Over the years I've learned to shift my way of thinking. While there may be times when people have accomplished extraordinary things and completed super human events, nevertheless, they are still human. They put their pants on one leg at a time, just like you and I. Essentially, we are all similar, cut from the same fabric and all gifted with the ability to succeed. While some of us may be talented in different areas, we all have the inborn capability and energy to accomplish great things.

But to do so, that inborn ability and energy must be cultivated in order to reach its full potential. Growing up, I had a dream of playing in the National Football League and following after the great running backs that came before my time. I often looked towards the players in the NFL for inspiration and motivation in my own life. And for me, one stood above the rest. His name was Emmitt Smith. Although he was considered to be undersized and not strong enough to succeed in the NFL, he eventually broke almost every major rushing record in NFL history. I idolized Smith. I didn't miss watching a game when he was playing. I studied everything about him. I wanted to be just like him on the field. I wanted to move like him, cut like him, follow blockers like him, and ultimately, be great just like him.

However, after my injury, it was another key player in the NFL who caught my interest. His name was Dennis Byrd. Not only did Dennis Byrd play in the NFL, but he also suffered a spinal cord injury and miraculously recovered to the point of being able to walk again. And to this day I am grateful to Dennis Byrd for doing that, because he gave me hope. For me, it was crucial to see someone recover from an accident as traumatic as the one I experienced.

Through Dennis, I found hope. There was no medical cure for the injury that I had. But Dennis Byrd lit a fire under my ass. I felt enormously motivated as I watched him walk onto a NFL football field after suffering such a debilitating injury. I knew in that moment that if he could do it, then so could I. I'm not sure what my motivation and determination level would have been had I not seen Dennis Byrd defeat his injury. It gave me hope to see another human being in a similar position. Sometimes seeing is really believing. Playing the role as a witness to Dennis Byrd was a pivotal moment in my recovery from my spinal cord injury. My drive to overcome my injury was triggered by my desire to break the constraints of being locked into a wheelchair for the rest of my life. But to see someone else do it was exactly what I needed to cement my own goals. Dennis pushed me to want to be an example to others to strive for whatever success they desire and not let the constraints, roadblocks, and debilitating situations of life keep them from experiencing the same success that I did. As a result, I began to look for opportunities where I could use my journey to overcome paralysis as an inspiration to others.

Upon my discharge from Lennox Baker Rehabilitation Center in Durham, North Carolina, I was scheduled to receive physical therapy at Cape Fear Valley Regional Medical Center in Fayetteville. The medical center was located about 30 minutes from my hometown in Lumberton and it was established that I would attend physical and occupational therapy three days a week after school. I was allowed to leave school early on those days. I was assigned to a very special physical therapist by the name of Pearl. Pearl specialized in the area of spinal cord injury rehabilitation. Upon my initial evaluation with Pearl, she inquired of my goals. I responded that I wanted to walk across the stage during my high school graduation. At this time it was January 1994. I was part of the 1996 graduation class, which meant I had 2 ½ years to accomplish this goal. Without a doubt, she believed in me. She believed that collectively, we could accomplish any goal. So our work began. She and another very special therapist, Valerie, immediately began exercises with me. Initially, I couldn't stand very long, but they kept at it. Pearl and Valerie implemented a rigorous therapeutic regimen. It was the most rigorous therapeutic regimen I had experienced since the accident. Most of the regimen included strengthening the muscles that were responsive to my commands. My favorite part of the regimen was actually walking. I was unable to advance my feet forward at the time, so one of the therapists had to do it for me. Because my objective was to walk across the stage, these ladies felt like the only way I could get there was to actually begin walking, even if it meant with their assistance. As a result, my entire therapeutic regimen was developed around walking again. It was not easy. There were many days that were very frustrating. The spinal cord does not heal like a cut or bruise. In my humble opinion, it is the slowest healing portion of the body. But that didn't stop us from working hard. Day in and day out, I put in the sweat equity to relearn how to walk and to retrain my mind and body to put one damn foot in front of the other. Graduation day arrived 2 ½ years later. I can remember sitting in my electric wheelchair, patiently waiting for my name to be called to receive my diploma. Once my name was called, Pearl graciously assisted me out of my wheelchair and onto my feet. She then handed me a walker and we attempted to take the steps leading up to the stage. With all of the strength I had inside of me, focusing on the fundamentals learned in physical therapy, I attempted to walk up the stairs on my own. It was very difficult and I needed assistance with each and every step. I kept trying and trying to move my legs. They did move some but not enough for me to clear the stairs. The audience was cheering me on. They were chanting my name and boosting me up.

I finally made it up the steps with the assistance of my therapist and my walker. I was able to make my way towards the podium and receive my diploma. As I looked out to the audience, I heard chanting, yelling and crying out. Many of my classmates were crying tears of joy, while some shed tears of inspiration and motivation. It was a very emotional moment. Although I felt like everything was taken away from me on that field, I was fighting to get it back.

As a result, my message for the class of 1996 was to strive wholeheartedly for success and to overcome any setbacks, obstacles, roadblocks, or hindrances standing in the way of that success. I wanted them to see my fight and watch me win my own personal battle. Perhaps I would be an example to them to fight, no matter what the odds may be. I thought of my goal of inspiring others while spending hours upon hours in physical therapy. Graduation night was an example to do just that. I had a heck of a support group and plenty of backers that rooted me on. In hindsight, the gift I gave to them in return was to succeed. Through overcoming my obstacles and reaching my personal goals, I am confident that I inspired many of my fellow classmates to face some of theirs. The same can be true for you. We can all be the inspiration that other people need. Remember that people are watching you intently when you act and when you react. There is no hiding it. So with that in mind, don't just do it for you; do it for those that need to see you do it. Get Up!

Chapter 4

SEEK OUT LIFE'S CHALLENGES

It is not easy to recover from a debilitating injury like severing your spinal cord. There were certainly times I thought I would never walk again. But, I did. I overcame a lot. However, that was yesterday and this is today. I refuse to just rest on my laurels and accomplishments. I firmly believe what is not challenged is not improved. So for me, learning how to walk again was just the first step. The next step is learning how to run. It is challenging the abilities I have obtained through physical therapy and taking it to the next level. It is great to wake up each and every morning with the opportunity to walk. But only if challenged can walking be improved.

Seeking out challenges means never taking the easy way out, but instead facing your fears and challenges to overcome them. Napoleon Hill said, "The path of least resistance makes all rivers and some men crooked." He also states, "There are no limitations to the mind except those we acknowledge." We are only limited to the challenges we are unwilling to overcome. Seeking out challenges means, regardless of the situation, being the aggressor towards life. It means remaining proactive and looking for or developing strategies that would be bulletproof and guarantee success. There are times when we can all sit back, relax, and rest on our laurels. In fact, I would tell you that all accomplishments should be acknowledged and celebrated, but never get so comfortable so as to stop moving forward.

To truly celebrate life, it is imperative to actively seek out life's challenges. They may be areas of weakness or those that you neglect to work on as a result of how they make you feel. They may make you uncomfortable or feel like a failure, but that is precisely why you can't simply ignore them. You should seek out these areas in your life with the purpose of improving them. Just as in the world of working out and staying fit, there may be a number of specific exercises you dislike or do not prefer. More times than not, it is because they are extremely challenging or push you beyond your comfort level. The reason why that particular exercise feels uncomfortable to you is likely because that area of emphasis needs attention and development. That particular area needs strengthening in order to develop the familiarity necessary for you to accomplish the exercise on a consistent and comfortable basis.

Similarly, there are areas in our life that fit the same type of scenario. Let's take the example of public speaking, as that can be a big fear for most people. Most people would simply avoid the opportunity of public speaking at all costs. But if we choose to live a life centered on welcoming and seeking out life's challenges, we'd dive head into this seemingly uncomfortable practice. It has been said that repetition is the first law of learning, thus the more you speak publicly and study your topic, the more comfortable you'll feel in front of an audience. But we can all agree that avoiding public speaking will never make you a better public speaker.

If fear is a challenge for you, this philosophy suggests that you consciously, actively, and consistently complete actions that require great courage on your part to overcome the challenge of fear. You actively seek out life's challenges by never ignoring the areas in which you are weak or uneasy. Instead, move these areas to the top of your consciousness and then develop strategies, routines, and habits that you can execute daily that will lead to you ultimately overcoming the weakness, fear, or challenge. Seeking out and overcoming life's challenges guarantees you will never settle for less and will always experience more. It puts you in control and in the driver's seat. Instead of bracing for the impact of life, it arms you with the ability to deliver the punches and pave the way towards your desired destiny. To be successful, we all must take the initiative. Success responds to the person that is consistent in his approach to overcome the demands of life. My family and others around me would not allow me to settle for life in a wheelchair. Initiated by a series of daily visits from Dr. Syvalla Washington and assisted by my dad and close friend and neighbor, Mr. William Breeden, Dr. Washington would stand me up and hand me a walker while praying for healing. Dr. Washington was and still is the Pastor and Spiritual Leader of Cromartie Temple of Praise. Their motto is to build a church "designed for and committed to the strengthening and deepening of the spiritual lives of its members, thereby enabling them to develop to the highest degree of spiritual endowment attainable in this life."

She demanded my body to stand and walk. While I stood there, holding onto my walker, everyone in the house concentrated and pushed me to take a step forward. Led by Dr. Washington and her missionaries, we all believed I would take a step before the end of the night and no one was willing to end the night without me doing just that. We developed a tremendous amount of faith through these evening rituals. We all believed that it could happen and we developed a strong desire for it to occur. As I attempted to advance my foot forward, Mr. Breeden would take his hands and literally pull each foot forward while chanting, "Come on Rodney, come on Rodney, Come on Rodney!!!" He motivated me and pushed me to believe that I could do it even when I could not.

Dr. Washington would also demand that I walk. Even when I couldn't do it, even when I didn't believe that I could do it, they had a strong desire for me to do it and they believed that I could. At times, my foot wouldn't move. They had to take the step for me, but eventually I took those first shaky steps. The muscle spasms were very active, and prevented my steps from being smooth and fluid. It took all the strength I had just to lift my leg, and eventually advance it.

In most cases, I was unable to lift my leg, and instead I advanced it by dragging my foot across the floor, but at that point I didn't care whether I was able to lift it or not. I was just glad to be able to move it at all. That one unsteady step turned into two and two into three and eventually, I was taking multiple steps. You could even say I was walking. Liberated by the fact that I could take a few steps, I knew that with continued effort I could take many steps and eventually step right out of my wheelchair. So I continued to take those steps each and every day. I accepted the challenge. Although I was able to finally take steps, my balance was horrible. The muscle tone in my legs made it very difficult to bend my leg at the knee and lift my leg up to advance it forward. Instead, the tightness of my thighs kept my leg in a very straight and rigid position, causing me to lean in a side-to-side manner to advance my foot forward. It was like watching a penguin walk.

However, a step was a step in my mind and this was a huge improvement from my initial accident. Realizing that this was a major accomplishment, I was eager to return to physical therapy to begin building upon the success. I knew that if it had taken over six months to barely take my first steps, I had a very long road ahead of me to independently walk again. Although doctors told me it was probably a slim chance that I would ever be able to walk on my own, dragging my foot forward offered me the needed confidence to keep going. It didn't matter whether they believed that or not. I was going to do this and my mind was made up. Walking again became a focus and my absolute desire above anything and everything else. I wanted nothing more than to be able to walk again. I wanted to spend all of my days and time in physical therapy working on walking. It became my obsession.

Eventually I learned to walk again. But the personal challenge had just begun. To ensure I was constantly improving, it was essential to seek out daily behaviors I could implement into my own life to draw closer to success. Success is a moving target. My definition changed by the day. Success first meant to stand up. Then it meant to move my foot. Then it meant to take just one step. Today, it means something completely different. Success means walking longer and accomplishing tasks quicker. I am constantly moving the chains and trying to tip the scales. One of the ways I implement this philosophy is by tracking how long it takes me to walk from the parking lot of my place of employment to my desk. That may seem like a simple task. In fact, I know I can accomplish it each and every day, but my goal is to do it faster and faster and faster with each attempt. I challenge myself to do better with every attempt.

The same should be true for you. We all have the opportunity and occasion to locate and welcome challenge into our lives. I am not talking about insurmountable challenges, but the little ones. The ones that make you a little stronger, quicker, faster, smarter, sharper, and closer to your goals. Success is the culmination of all the challenges we overcome. Joseph Campbell said, "Opportunities to find deeper powers within ourselves come when life seems most challenging." My opportunities come from challenging myself to become more agile and mobile. That is a challenge I choose to seek each and every day of my own life.

So, what's your challenge? What do you work towards improving on a daily basis? It is likely not your ability to walk, but do you challenge yourself to be a better friend? Father? Mother? Husband? Wife? Employee? Leader? Cook? Coach? The options are vast. The only mistake you can make is not seeking enough challenges in your own life.

Chapter 5

Be Willing to Do Whatever it Takes

When you really want something in life, you will do whatever it takes to get what you want. There might be obstacles, challenges, and seemingly impossible hurdles to overcome, but you will charge, full speed ahead, because you know in your heart it is worth the outcome. Yes, there will be setbacks, but you can't let your fear of failure hold you back from achieving your goals. When you feel strongly about something, your feelings will turn into actions, and your actions will lead you to the very things you desire.

We all have the ability to do great things in life and accomplish our dreams, if we are only willing to do what it takes to turn our dreams into reality. Turning dreams into reality requires us to take action, and work towards our goals. In my opinion, it is the difference between those who live their dreams and those who only dream. For me, it certainly was the difference between being able to walk again, rather than living my life confined to a wheelchair.

But some people fail to realize their dreams simply because they're not willing to do what it takes to succeed. Those who succeed never settle for less and never choose to take the easiest path ahead. Those on the road towards success understand that the path of least resistance often leads to a destination filled with failure or mediocrity. Instead, successful people find out exactly what is necessary in order for them to reach the highest level of success, and choose to complete the steps necessary to reach that level. Regardless of the challenge ahead, if you want to be successful you must conduct the proper research to find out what is absolutely necessary to succeed. Once the research is complete, you must be willing to execute the steps you have discovered in order to reach your desired destination. Essentially, you should be willing to do whatever it takes.

Maintaining a willingness to do whatever it takes is a two-step process that involves first making a decision and then taking action (whatever that action may be) to achieve the desired outcome. You cannot take steps towards reaching a goal without first making the decision. As Vince Lombardi says, "The difference between a successful person and others is not a lack of strength, not a lack of knowledge, but rather a lack of will." Once the decision is made, action follows as a result of that decision. However, you must maintain the decision to reach your goals in order to sustain the necessary action, effort, and endurance required to experience that same goal.

Although I felt a sense of accomplishment upon getting through the first three weeks of rehab and finally being able to contract a muscle in my leg, I was frustrated at the amount of time that had passed leading up to that point. The reality of my battle began to set in as I came to the realization that my recovery was not going to happen fast. It was going to take a lot of hard work and determination, but above all it was going to take a lot of patience. Thoughts of wanting to give up attempted to invade my mind, but I refused to let the thoughts get in the way of my progress; I wanted so much more. Robert Kiyosaki says, "The size of your success is measured by the strength of your desire; the size of your dream; and how you handle disappointment along the way." Although I wasn't going to heal as fast as I desired, this disappointment wasn't going to make me give up. I was designed to be on the football field, and that is where I wanted to be. I wanted my life back. I felt like someone had come in and robbed me of my own life. Therefore, I had to do something about it.

Another area of focus within my rehabilitation was in measuring my size and body weight in preparation for me to move around in a wheelchair of my own. During this stage of my recovery, the therapists did not consider a manual wheelchair for my specific injury. They measured and fitted me for an electric wheelchair; one that you drive around with a joystick. Believe it or not, there were questions and concerns of whether I would even be able to operate a joystick. Although I did regain some movement in my shoulders and in my triceps, I was pretty weak. I did not have any dexterity in my hands and was unable to grip the joystick. Instead I would motion my arm over the joystick in order to operate it from left to right, or back and forth. I had to learn how to operate the electric wheelchair with the aid of the physical therapist because I just could not move much at all. I felt as though I was living a nightmare over and over and over again. It was literally dangerous to be in the same room with me as I attempted to maneuver the chair as I was bumping into things and running over personal property in the rehabilitation gym. It was somewhat hilarious to others, but absolutely debilitating to me.

I hated every aspect of being in that wheelchair. Staff members (as well as others) would often times joke with me and say that I could pick up girls and have them sit on my lap while taking them on joyrides. All of that sounded fine and dandy to them, but their comedy was my reality. In this case, I could not get out of the wheelchair. My days were spent just sitting in the chair and riding around, which was extremely unfulfilling. I'm sure the nurses and the medical staff at the rehabilitation center could see how I felt by the expressions on my face, but I never mumbled or complained. Instead, after all of my physical and occupational sessions, tests, appointments, and personal medical schedules were completed, I would ask the medical staff to put me in a manual chair. I would ask that they push me to the end of the hallway, far away from my room, so that I could attempt to push myself back.

I figured that pushing the chair would only help me get stronger and possibly strengthen the grip and dexterity in my hands to allow me to be more independent. The hallway was approximately 100 yards or about a football field long. It took me over two hours to make it to my room during my first several attempts. Although frustrated and saddened by my lack of mobility, I did not let this deter me from my end goal. I was determined to push the chair down the hall and into my room. I was not going to allow myself to be taken out of the chair until I made it to my room, no matter how long it took. I had made that commitment to myself and I told the medical staff that this was the way it was going to be, no matter what. I was going to make it into my room every single time I got in that wheelchair. I would have to take short breaks in order to allow my arms and shoulders to rest and recover just so that I could try again. This process would repeat itself several times over before I would make it into my room.

I will admit, there were some days that I did not make it into my room. Some of those days involved me just not having enough strength to go the distance. My strength level varied depending upon the types of activities that were required during my physical and occupational therapy sessions throughout the day. There were times when certain individuals on the medical staff just could not stand to see me struggle in the chair and would come get me, despite my reluctance to quit. However, the very next day I would get right back in the chair and do it all over again.

Despite the difficulty of pushing the chair, I improved over the course of time. My shoulders and arms grew stronger as a result of pushing the wheelchair every day. By the time I left the rehabilitation center, I was able to push a wheelchair for 50 yards or more; but I was still dependent on the use of an electric wheelchair for most of my days. I could have let this deter me, but instead, I just kept my focus on working towards only using a manual wheelchair. I had made my decision, which meant I just had to keep acting upon it to reach my goal. I was going to do whatever it took to get stronger. I followed the words of Booker T. Washington: "Success is to be measured not so much by the position that one has reached in life as by the obstacles which he has overcome."

Doing whatever it takes is an indication that you have made the decision in your mind to take whatever action is necessary to experience your desired outcome. It means you have created a spiritual, mental, and emotional environment of self-determination and motivation to press forward with whatever ideas, strategies or plans you've defined necessary to accomplish a goal. Not only does this decision put you on a path towards your goal, it also strengthens your spiritual and mental muscles. If channeled positively, being willing to do whatever it takes promises a step up from your current condition. However, if channeled negatively, you could get involved in behaviors and activities that are not for a good cause. Instead of bringing value to your life, this behavior could cause destruction and sorrow. Implementing the principle of doing whatever it takes requires good judgment. For me, the distinction between positive and negative determinations was an answer to just one question that I would ask myself at any given moment to rebalance my thoughts, feelings, and emotions: "Are the activities, behaviors, thoughts, and feelings I'm currently experiencing on a daily basis drawing me closer to my desired outcome, or are they pushing me away from my desired goal?"

I encourage you to use this question to evaluate whether or not doing whatever it takes is going to help you reach your goal. There will be times when you decide that doing whatever it takes isn't worth it, and that is okay. It took me a long time to take the first step and decide that I was willing to do whatever it took to strengthen my body, heal my emotions, and get my life back. I certainly did not feel that way in the beginning.

Honestly, I was mad at the world and full of resentment for being in a wheelchair. Oftentimes I asked, "Why me? Why is it that I have suffered such a traumatizing and debilitating injury in my life?" I wondered why I couldn't have just suffered some type of shoulder injury, or knee injury. You know, one that would allow me to fully recover. Why did my injury have to be life threatening? I had a vision of the way I wanted to live my life prior to my accident. I wanted to be very active in sports, maintain a muscular and athletic physique, and be the kind of guy that was very skilled at using my hands such as making home repairs, auto repairs, and completing any type of task that involved physical activity. Prior to my accident, you could say I never sat still; I was always busy doing something. If I wasn't working out, I was washing cars or mowing the lawn or doing something that required full physical ability. Upon suffering my injury, I was introduced to wheelchairs, and adaptive equipment that I was encouraged to use in order to execute daily activities such as dressing and bathing. For many reasons, I was against the use of a wheelchair and adaptive equipment. It made me feel belittled and helpless. It actually humiliated me to not only have lost my physical ability, but also to have to use ugly and pervasive tools to assist myself with daily activities. It made me feel as though I was abnormal because I required special treatment. That feeling made me not want to live at all. It made me not want to face the reality of my injury. It made me want to die. I hated every aspect of the experience. Having to sit in the wheelchair all day was just one aspect of it, as there were several additional consequences that accompanied my spinal cord injury. I hated having to deal with all of the personal exposure, medical requirements, appointments, and evaluations. After returning home from living in the hospital for four months and not experiencing any significant return that would indicate I would fully recover from the accident, I felt like the world was against me. I wanted to run away from it all, but everywhere I went, evidence of this debilitating injury followed me in the form of my own personal wheelchair and the inability to physically move

Mentally stressed, and emotionally strained, I spent several days outside sitting in my electric wheelchair, contemplating suicide. Often times I would wheel myself away from my house to the closest busiest street and wait for an 18-wheeler to come storming by so I could roll out in front of the truck and get it all over with. Only the thought of somehow surviving this incident, and suffering physical injuries much worse than what my body was currently experiencing, stopped me from executing the plan.

Those thoughts made me realize that I had to create a more positive and life producing plan to overcome this injury. I realized that the plan I was considering was the easy way out. It was the most effortless conceivable plan to get rid of the injury. However, it still would not get me what I wanted. It would not allow for me to live the life I wanted to live. As a matter of fact, that plan would take away all possible opportunities of success and potential possibilities of recovery. It was a sure way to lose the game of life and allow the effects of this injury to defeat me personally, physically, spiritually, emotionally, and mentally.

Even though the odds were not in my favor, fighting back and attempting to regain my physical function and live a productive life gave me a possibility of success; a possibility of walking again; a possibility of living a happy and fulfilled life, and that possibility, as small as it was, was enough for me to say "I'm willing to do whatever it takes to experience that success as small as it may be."

That small percentage of possibility became my burning desire. It became my dream. It became everything that I wanted in life. It became my vision and my goal. I wanted nothing more than to experience that, and as a result, I was willing to do whatever it took to experience that piece of success. I had made my decision to live the life I wanted, and I would start to take action to make my dream a reality. As Pablo Picasso says, "Action is the key to all success." Once I set my intention, I knew there was no turning back. Take my determination and use it as inspiration to set your own goals. Is there something you want to accomplish? Make the decision to achieve your goal, and start taking action to make your dream a reality.

Chapter 6

Ignite the Small Accomplishments

An accomplishment is that moment when you experience a desired outcome, or when you have finally reached a goal. The bliss of accomplishment includes any type of improvement (big or small) to yourself, others, or a particular situation. When feeling accomplished, we are able to perceive the results we desire. However, accomplishment doesn't come easy; you have to work for it, and this is one of the reasons why it is so satisfying. When we finally enjoy the fruits of our labor, we know all the hard work was worth it, and we are inspired to start anew. As Harvey Mackay says, "A great accomplishment shouldn't be the end of the road, just the starting point for the next leap forward." There is an endless amount of potential accomplishments towards which we can work. Often times we focus on achieving the overall goal and neglect to understand the significance of the small accomplishments. Our experience along the journey becomes solely focused on the overall objective. What we must remember is that the small steps are the ones that, when added up, allow us to reach our prime goal.

In the words of Lao-tzu, "A journey of a thousand miles begins with a single step." When traveling from point A to point B, it is the small accomplishments in between the two points that allow us to reach our desired destination. Without having completed and executed the steps in between, we would never find success.

Think about a time when you experienced a great accomplishment in your life. As you dwell back on the past, it's not only the accomplishment that comes to mind—it is also the journey along the way. Take the time to appreciate the not-so-significant events, the people, and the small accomplishments that occurred during the journey that allowed you to reach the "great accomplishment." These are the building blocks to success, for it is in these moments that decisions occur. As a result of these decisions, we achieve small accomplishments and we start to build one achievement upon the other, which causes growth in our personality, spiritual connection, and emotional being.

Amidst these moments of accomplishment, there will also be times when we fail. However, we learn from these moments that there is much to gain. In most cases, these moments either build or destroy our faith and confidence. Some people tend to get frustrated with failure and quit. Vince Lombardi advises, "The greatest accomplishment is not in never falling, but in rising again after you fall." This is exactly why we must understand that it is within these moments that the real heroes are made. Failure is inevitable; the key is getting back up and trying again until we succeed.

What I love about small accomplishments is that they allow for a sense of reward along the way to your overall objective. You don't have to wait until the end to celebrate! There's plenty to get excited about when accomplishing small, but significant, events that are going to align with you reaching your overall goal. During the time that I was a Contracting Officer for the United States Navy, there was a lot of emphasis placed on executing the acquisition process, and ultimately reaching the contract award in a timely fashion. There was a significant amount of attention and focus placed on meeting the desired need dates in order to avoid negative impacts to the fleet. However, in order to meet the desired contract award date, there were many steps within the acquisition process that had to occur. Whenever the acquisition team was successful at executing the final contract award in accordance with fleet requirements, it was celebrated and acknowledged. However, there were many steps we had to take in order to reach that final contract date.

I always felt that we should have not only celebrated the final contract award, but also praised the small accomplishments within the acquisition process. This would have allowed us to focus on the progression towards the overall objective. It is the small accomplishments that have to be completed in order for the overall objective to be realized, which is why in some ways they are more important than the overall goal. First, we must define what we want, and then we must define what has to be done in order to achieve it. At that point, what has to be done is more important than what we want, simply because if we don't do what has to be done, we're not going to get or experience what we desire. Leonardo da Vinci once said, "It had long since come to my attention that people of accomplishment rarely sat back and let things happen to them. They went out and happened to things." We have to take action if we want to see results.

During my spinal injury recovery at Duke Medical Center, I often received visits from my good friend, Dr. Washington. During one of her visits she asked me to do something that I had not been able to do just after the accident: She asked me to wiggle my fingers. Attempting to fulfill her request, for the first time since the date of my accident, there was movement and twitching of my fingers. I was so astonished by this minor movement that I began to cry tears of joy. The movement in my fingers was something that I could work with—it was a starting point for my larger recovery goals. Expecting more, Dr. Washington repositioned herself at the foot of my bed and asked me to wiggle my toes. Although very faint and twitchy, for the very first time since the date of my accident, I was able to wiggle the toes of my left foot. I tried very hard to move the toes of my right foot, but they would not budge. However, I was overjoyed, along with the pastor and my mother, by the fact that there was movement in my extremities I had not yet experienced.

I consider this a very crucial moment in my road to recovery as it increased my faith and gave me a platform to begin my journey. As far as I was concerned, my body had given me an indication that it was healing itself. It was a small accomplishment, but I knew there were many more to come. The road ahead would be full of hard work before I would reach my larger goal, but these small accomplishments would carry me there in time.

I thanked Dr. Washington for making the two-hour trip to visit me. As she exited my room, she assured me that I hadn't seen the last of her. She advised my mother to keep her updated on all the latest and greatest reports regarding my recovery. She also wanted to know the date of my dismissal, and when I would be coming home so she could visit more often. As she was walking out the door she looked back at me and said, "We're going to get you up and walking when you get home." It was the most positive thing I had heard since the date of my injury. Without knowing how it was going to happen, I looked forward to going home and getting up and walking.

The next morning, I shared my experience with my physical and occupational therapists by demonstrating the newfound movement in my fingers and toes. They were absolutely astonished and amazed by the twitching. Immediately they transferred me to the exercise mat and began more electronic therapy. We focused on the areas of my hands and feet in order to further jumpstart the recovery process in my extremities. The idea was to continue to train the nervous system to receive and transmit the signals down to the areas below the level of injury. I didn't change my normal routine of pushing my wheelchair every day after my therapeutic sessions, however I added additional strategies and exercises, such as twitching my fingers and toes 200 times a day. None of my therapists knew that I was doing this, and they did not recommend it, but I figured if I continued to do it then I would strengthen my toes and fingers to a point where I could use them functionally. After about four weeks I noticed I could actually squeeze and hold the phone in the palm of my hand. Before then, someone had to prop the phone up against my face so I could communicate with the person on the other line. When no one was available to help with the phone, the nursing aids strapped Velcro to my hands and also to the phone to allow me to pick up the phone whenever I received a call.

However, as a result of implementing the strategy of twitching my fingers several times a day, my hands were getting stronger. I was able to grip the hand rims of the wheelchair a lot better than when I first started, which allowed me to complete a stronger push and advance the wheelchair a little faster. I also noticed that my triceps were getting stronger as a result of pushing the wheelchair every day. Several weeks later I had decreased the time it took to push down the hallway by 15 minutes.

Although very small in nature, these gains and accomplishments motivated me to keep trying. I would bring exercise bands and balls with me from therapy to play with while sitting in my hospital room. I remained outside of bed as much as possible, and even though it meant sitting up in my wheelchair most of the time, I felt it was better than lying in bed. My mind was always focused on doing something that would help me get better, stronger, or faster. I often asked my therapist for recommendations and exercises I could execute whenever I was not in therapy. Both the physical and occupational therapists were impressed by my work ethic and positive attitude. One even mentioned to my family that it was very rare to find a person so motivated and determined to fight against an injury as traumatizing and debilitating as the one I experienced. They went on to state that it takes a lot of determination, support, and faith to overcome such an injury. I think it also takes a belief that the small accomplishments will eventually lead to the big ones.

I am a living testament to the belief that small accomplishments are the building blocks for a larger creation of success. We do not experience great success by chance; it is deliberate and repetitive small successes that lead to great success. As Wallace D. Wattles says, "There is no such thing as chance. Everything happens according to the law. Nothing in the entire universe ever happens, unless it occurs according to the law. Nothing ever escapes the law." Igniting, focusing, and ultimately completing small accomplishments will, by law, lead to great success. You just have to take the steps necessary to find those small accomplishments. No accomplishment should stand on its own. Instead, it should be used to help accomplish larger achievements, and even after it has exhausted its use, accomplishments remain a reminder of what we can achieve, and therefore serve as encouragement to maintain, or gain, the faith and confidence necessary for greatness.

People need only to look at their lives in order to recognize the small accomplishments that have already occurred. Oftentimes, our idea of success is so big that we forget that success is only a compilation of small accomplishments, some of which we have already experienced. We can now begin to build upon those accomplishments and move towards our desired goals. Living a life filled with small accomplishments first begins with an inventory of all of the positive, remarkable, and outstanding things about ourselves. In defining these assets, we can start to identify how to use them to reach our goals. In order to do this, we must have faith that it can be done, and be willing to take the lessons learned from previous chapters in order to make it happen. Richard Bach advises, "You are never given a dream without also being given the power to make it true. You may have to work for it, however." When we decide to put in the hard work necessary to reach our goals, we can celebrate the small accomplishments and experience great success.

Chapter 7

ALWAYS PUSH
YOURSELF TO LEVELS
ABOVE THE SOCIAL
AVERAGE

The social average is what is normally expected from an individual in today's society. In the US, it is typically expected for you to graduate from high school, go to college, get good grades, get a degree, obtain a job, purchase a house, have children, and work until you retire, hopefully with enough money to take care yourself and your family for the remainder of your life. We call this the "American Dream." Luckily, people are starting to realize there is more to life than hitting the social average. When you strive for less than what you are worth, you will never reach your full potential. We all must be willing to set higher goals and follow through with the action necessary to achieve our dreams. As J. Cole wisely observed, "I always feel like it's two key ingredients when it comes to following your dreams, making something happen that the average person deems difficult. If you truly believe it, that's step one. Step two, is, you know, the hard work that goes along with it." Yes, you will have to work hard, but the reward will be the best life that you can imagine.

The American dream suggests that you have a job and work that job until you retire. But, in today's world, this formula is rapidly changing. There are plenty of people who earn money, way beyond what a 9 to 5 job can pay, and don't even have a 9 to 5 job. Conversely, a lot people have the goal of working a 9 to 5 job for the rest of their lives, and are completely happy with that scenario. There is nothing wrong with someone who chooses to live all his life working in the social average; it does not make you any less of a person.

However, I believe that there's a better way, a much more fulfilling way of living—a life above what is socially acceptable. One could call it a rich life or wealthy one, even though it isn't measured by money at all.

People don't have to make the decision to work all of their life. They can choose to retire young. They can choose to live a life filled with like-minded friends and enjoy the freedom to travel the world, experience exotic foods, dress themselves with the best of fabrics, and experience a side of life not available to those that settle for what is just socially acceptable. Attaining this life requires you to push beyond that level of social acceptance, and into the realm of dreaming. This will open the floodgates of opportunity not known to those who do not seek it. Those that want more must seek it. Those who want to live above what's socially acceptable should become aware of the existence and availability of a better life, so that they have the ability to make it their own.

Living a life above the social average brings about great success to all involved. The results can change the lives of many. It can put you in a place where you're able to help others you otherwise would not be able to help. Living a life above the social average can be an example to others to strive for more, to do more, to seek more, to believe more, and to experience more. Living a life above the social average opens up the possibility of living your best life; life with less worry and less stress, and with more happiness, joy, creativity and experience.

Pushing yourself beyond the social average takes effort, persistence, endurance, and internal strength. Most people will find it very challenging to step off the road of normalcy and into the path of uncertainty. There is a level of risk you must push beyond in order to experience the benefits of living a full life.

However, this is where the magic happens. It is written in The Bible, "to whom much is given, much is required." It is what's required of an individual who decides to push beyond the social average that makes the difference. Just as pushing against an unmovable rock for a long period of time produces and strengthens muscle, pushing against the social average builds character, internal strength, faith, courage, and other characteristics necessary to live a rich life.

By pushing yourself above what is socially acceptable, you learn how to obtain your goals through trial and error. In doing so, you become aware of the process, tools, information and knowledge necessary to never have to worry about living a life below what is most fulfilling, abundant, rich, wealthy, and economically acceptable to you. Not only will you never settle for anything again, you also will develop knowledge that you can share with someone else, so they too can experience greatness. The material and financial gains that you experience not only benefit you, but also change the lives of others, who in turn can create a domino effect of individuals who no longer settle for less, but demand more from life and teach others to do the same. What a wonderful world we can create with this mindset and behavior.

After my injury, the social average was no longer an option for my life. I quickly fell below it. At one point, it was unexpected for me to even graduate from high school. No one expected me to be able to drive a car or live on my own. It was a long shot for me to enter the workforce at all. What was expected was that I would barely avoid the confines of the rest home, and live in an apartment attached to my mother's house so that my family could care for me. It was anticipated that I would spend the rest of my life confined to an electric wheelchair. It was anticipated that I would never recover from the traumatic and debilitating emotional impact of the injury I suffered. It was expected that I would have no reason to smile and or be happy; that all of my days I would be filled with depression and emotionally strained as a result of the injury.

While I was in the hospital, I was visited by numerous medical professionals, each specific to a particular area of medicine. All were members of a rehabilitation team designed to help me develop the strategies I would need to address the changes in my body caused by the spinal injury. Areas of focus included bladder control, bowel control, skin sensation, circulatory control, respiratory function, muscle tone, fitness and wellness, sexual health, pain, and depression. As a result, I not only had a neurosurgeon assigned to me, but also had a urologist, physical and occupational therapists, a chaplain, a speech therapist, a respiratory therapist, dermatologists, and a psychologist.

Each of these specialists gave me rules to follow and medicine to take to control the negative side effects of my injury and prevent further complications in each of these areas. No longer was I thinking about what to major in when I went to college; instead, I was trying to remember to empty my bladder every four hours to prevent infection, and move my body every couple of hours to prevent pressure sores. It was the most debilitating feeling ever. In addition, the doctors warned that I may never get off the medication, and suggested that my family and I prepare for my life to include these medications and other adaptations necessary for me to live. The doctors also advised on all the necessary equipment that I would need in order to make my life easier. In turn, we had to consider making alterations to our current living space to accommodate my needs. The doctors and the physical therapists wanted to know the layout of my current living conditions in order to determine what type of things I would need to learn to be independent at home. Needless to say, it was very overwhelming for everyone involved. We didn't know how to deal with in injury like this; my parents were average working-class people who had been thrown a curveball. We lived in a very small home. We all contemplated whether my wheelchair would fit in our home without causing damage. Life had been turned upside down for all of us. At a certain point, I realized that the social average had been redefined for my life, and so I started to redefine my goals. I would have to push beyond what was thought possible for my life, and strive for even bigger accomplishments.

For example, no one thought it was possible for me to be able to drive a vehicle again after my injury. However, as you can imagine, I had a burning desire to regain my ability to drive. I had suffered my injury only days after receiving my learner's permit, so I hadn't spent much time behind the wheel, but boy was I eager. I was looking forward to driving to school and to the sporting events, and going out on dates or just hanging out with friends. Instead, I was rolling around in an electric wheelchair I could barely control. Even after regaining the strength to push a manual wheelchair, I was chauffeured to and from doctor's appointments and all other events.

However, my burning desires to drive myself around and experience that sense of independence never subsided. Instead it grew to a point that pushed me beyond what was expected to achieve that which I desired. Even though it was unlikely for me to be able to drive as a result of my injury, I did the research to find out who could teach me how to drive and what adaptive equipment I needed in order to do so. I obtained a license to drive and continue to drive today. I've used several versions of adaptive equipment since I began operating a vehicle, but today, the only adaptive equipment I need is a simple hand control.

Furthermore, it was unexpected that I would ever finish high school after my injury. My injury occurred on the third day of my sophomore year of high school. Doctor's didn't think that I would regain the strength and mobility to return to high school. It was uncertain how I was going to continue my education. Not only did I graduate from high school, but I also obtained a Master's degree later on in life. I did not accept the "average" that was expected for my recovery. I did not accept the limitations that were placed on me because of my condition. I was determined to rise above my injury and follow my dreams. As a result, I achieved my dreams and even more. But perhaps the greatest example and achievement is that I no longer require the use of a wheelchair, but instead I walk around my workplace and within my community with my own two legs. I no longer take all of the prescribed medications. Nowadays, I give my body the essentials it needs to form a solid nutritional foundation via ultra-premium blend of 12 full-spectrum vitamins, plant-sourced minerals, whole-fruit mangosteen, organic glyconutrient-rich aloe vera and organic green tea called VEMMA. (For more information please visit www. Myhealthdrinks. Com) But most rewarding is how I've inspired and touched the lives of thousands of people, helped them overcome obstacles, and inspired them to achieve their dreams and live their lives to the fullest. All because of pushing beyond what was expected of me.

Pushing yourself above the social norm first begins with a dream: Your dream. A clearly defined chain of what you want your life to be. What do you want out of life? What type of car do you want? What type of house do you want to live in? What kind of family do you want to have? How much money do you want to make? What type of vacations do you want to take? What destinations do you want to see? What type of relationship do you want? Honestly answering these questions is the starting point of pushing beyond the social average. You must be able to fully define and describe what is it you want. Please note, I did not ask what is it that you are willing to accept, but rather what is it that you want. This should be a clearly defined idea that you conceptualize and visualize and then write down on paper. This is the first step because you must have a reason to push, a reason not to settle for less. Your dream, mixed with a strong desire to experience it, should increase the level of determination that will allow you to implement the next step of developing a plan. Find out everything that is necessary and required in order for you to realize your dream. Learn whatever you need to learn. Talk to someone who's done it before, so that he can show you what has to be done. Go after your dreams wholeheartedly, and do not settle for less.

Believe that you will achieve your goals and visualize your dreams on a regular basis. Keep the dream in front of you, and make sure the steps you are taking are bringing you closer every day. In the words of Anatole France, "To accomplish great things, we must not only act, but also dream; not only plan, but also believe." Visualize yourself as if you already accomplished your dream, and imagine what it will feel like. Once you accomplish those dreams, feel and embrace the accompanying emotions. Practice excellence in all that you do and don't let anything shake your faith. You are better than average—believe this so you can get up and live a rich, satisfying, and fulfilling life.

Chapter 8

DEMAND MORE FROM YOURSELF THAN ANYONE ELSE DOES

Demanding more from yourself than anyone else means never settling for the expectations others may place on you, and instead, placing expectations and demands on yourself that far exceed what anyone could ever possibly expect. It means going over and above what's required. It means going the extra mile and potentially another mile, if necessary. As Sam Walton says, "High expectations are the key to everything." Demanding more means living a life of excellence by succeeding in all of your endeavors, and not settling for anything less than the best. Give the best of what you have to offer in all you do and be willing to give even more when your best is not good enough.

Achieving your goal at all costs means focusing in on your desire for success and not letting go until it is realized in your life. It requires placing high demands on yourself in order to achieve your desires. Prior to my accident, when I trained for football in high school, I would find work out strategies and regiments that were designed for athletes at the collegiate level. Although I was a high school football athlete, I demanded that I performed at a level above my current abilities. I felt this strategy would give me an edge over my colleagues. I wanted to learn more about the game, and more about work out techniques and strategies that were somewhat more advanced than my level of play. Once I learned what those advanced techniques and strategies were, I executed and performed to that level.

Demanding more from yourself than anyone else does is all about seeking and demanding an output over and above what is required. Do more than enough, not for someone else but for your own satisfaction. It is crossing the finish line at full speed instead of dragging yourself across, if at all.

Demanding more allowed me to reach my goals; it has been the foundation and the stepping-stone for success in every area of my life. Demanding more put me in a position to write this book and present my personal story to you. There is no cure for a significant spinal cord injury. Upon suffering such a debilitating injury, I had no choice but to rely on my genetics to heal. Upon any nerve regeneration or functional return that occurs over the course of recovery, demands must be placed on that return of function in order to strengthen the body and retrain the nervous system to make that function permanent. It is not easy. It seems as if gravity, and everything else for that matter, is against you. But, you must place demands on your body to function. Even when you don't want to or you don't feel like it, you have to do it. I have forced myself out of bed in order to practice dressing myself, bathing myself, walking, and pushing a wheelchair.

I expected more of myself than anyone else did for years on end, 18 to be exact, before I was able to become completely independent of a wheelchair. Upon my initial injury, I didn't know how life was going to turn out for me. My doctors and physical therapists made all types of projections based on my level of function and strength at that time, but those were their expectations based on their knowledge and evaluations. I created my own vision of what I wanted my life to look like in 5 years, 10 years, and 20 years from the date of my accident. Never did I accept what the doctors and the physical therapists told me. I knew they were smart, but they had no idea how much desire I had inside. I didn't know how I was going to create the life that I visualized in my mind, but I knew that I was going to do it, no matter what.

The doctors wanted me to function at a level that would allow me to be independent despite my personal injury. They wanted to teach me how to live life in a wheelchair, with a C5/C6 spinal cord injury. As I went about executing the strategies and routines and regiments required in order for me to meet the expectations of my doctors, I placed demands on myself that went far beyond what the doctors prescribed. I demanded more of myself because I wanted out of that wheelchair. I placed high demands on myself so that I could live the life of my dreams. If they told me to walk 100 feet, I would walk 200. If 200 feet was the goal for the day, I shot for 400. Their goals were always lower than the ones I set for myself.

I wanted to be a part of conversations about fitness and working out, and contribute by talking about my workout regimen. There were several times when I requested a more intense rehabilitation regimen, and was admitted into the hospital for a period of 2 to 3 months in order to receive intense physical therapy. Upon my request, this type of rehab included aquatic therapy, intense physical training, and very focused occupational rehabilitation geared toward regaining strength, functionality, and independence. Despite the odds, I was on a mission to win the war, to escape the confines of a wheelchair, and live a life filled with happiness and success despite my disability. I could've sat at home and collected a disability check, but that would've been so unfulfilling. I wanted more for myself. There were things in life that I wanted to see. Places I wanted to go. A life I wanted to create and live, but most of all, I wanted to contribute.

The desires that I had for life would not allow me to settle for anything less than the mental picture I visualized daily. I was going to stop at nothing. I knew that if I was going to be successful and compete with able-bodied people, I had to have an edge that would always be my work ethic and determination.

My initial time in rehab was rather depressing. My gains were slow and small. In most cases it seemed as if I wasn't making any gains at all. After four weeks in rehab, it still took over an hour for me to make it down the hallway and back to my room in a manual wheelchair. But I was ready to take it to the next level. I wanted to see some dramatic changes that gave me an indication that I was healing. I wanted to begin taking steps without assistance. I wanted to begin lifting my arms above my head and holding them there. I wanted to begin pushing the wheelchair fast, so I would some-times imagine feeling the wind against my face as a result of swiftly pushing the wheelchair. However that was not my story. Not at that moment. Instead, I needed around-the-clock 24-hour care.

Using the aid of an arm sling and an adaptive fork allowed me to feed myself, but I wasn't 100% efficient at doing so. Picking up a cup to drink was impossible without spilling it all over myself. I used an adaptive spoon for soups and cereals, but I didn't have the stability in my arm, shoulders, or hands to keep the spoon steady, so most of the liquid I scooped in the spoon would spill out before I could get it to my mouth. I found this to be very frustrating because I would go through the entire process of feeding myself, and spilling everything all over myself, only to ask someone to help me complete the process.

My mother could see the frustration that this caused me. Being a Christian, she would always talk to me about God and how he could heal me. She tried to remain strong, but I could see the pain and agony my injury created. She posted Bible verses and inspirational quotes on the wall next to my bed. One of my favorites is, "I can do all things through Christ who strengthens me." The power of God was all that we had. The only thing the doctors recommended was that I continue to go to rehab and to prepare for 24-hour care for the rest of my life. No one in my family wanted that. Therefore, no one believed that. We were not willing to accept it. The Scriptures and inspirational quotes on the wall were my mother's way of making sure that I did not give up. I studied the Scriptures and quotes day and night. I committed them to memory and I would whisper them to myself during my therapy sessions as I tried to move my legs or arms.

Demanding more from myself than anyone else does has put me in the position to be an inspiration for others. People see my story as an indication that anything is possible for those that believe and are willing to place demands on themselves in order to get the results they desire. At times my journey serves as an epiphany to others, and dilutes the excuses most people use for not reaching their goals and living a life they desire. I think sometimes I'm symbolic of the effort required to reach a goal. I'm symbolic of that effort that some people are not willing to put forward. I think people see me and realize that if this guy can do it, surely they can do it too. As Ralph Marston says, "Don't lower your expectations to meet your performance. Raise your level of performance to meet your expectations. Expect the best of yourself, and then do what is necessary to make it a reality." Demanding more from yourself than anyone else will not be easy, but it will push you to work hard and be the best version of yourself possible. Dream big, and then get up and put in the effort necessary to make those dreams come true.

Chapter 9

TIRED? DO IT ANYWAY

To most, being tired is a physical, emotional, or mental feeling. But it can also be a state of mind. When we are tired, we are faced with a choice. We can allow the feeling to defeat us, or depending upon the demand of the situation, we can command the body to continue pressing forward until we complete the task and reach our goals. Thus, we have to know when our bodies and minds truly need to rest. We need to recognize when the body/mind/spirit need to rejuvenate, and we must then grant ourselves the permission to embrace the necessary stillness to achieve that end. In many cases, we use being tired as an excuse to stop, and discontinue the press forward towards our goals and dreams. As Vince Lombardi observes, "Fatigue makes cowards of us all." If you are not aware, being tired can rob you of the very thing you desire most in your life.

In so many ways, being tired was my body's way of telling me it did not want to move on. On many occasions, my body wanted to quit. Not only did my body want to quit, but my mind and emotions were also frustrated and tired of all the nuances and debilitating side effects as a result of my injury. My body was always telling me to surrender. There were days when I felt too tired to even get out of bed. Too tired to push my wheelchair. Too tired to do anything that required physical activity.

I had to discipline myself on a daily basis and create new behavior that would lead me towards success. As human beings, we have a tendency to want to quit whenever we feel the burn. So whenever

I felt tired or frustrated, I would ask myself, "What will I do to get myself out of this wheelchair and live the life I desire?" My answer to that question: "Any and everything that will draw me closer to walking again."

Henry David Thoreau said, "If one advances confidently in the direction of his dreams, and endeavors to live the life which he has imagined, he will meet with a success unexpected in common hours." I knew I could not stop. I had to keep going—tired, frustrated, fatigued, I had to put forward the effort in order to achieve my goals. Similar to a magnet, I had to move towards my goal in order to attract it into my life.

Moving towards my goal meant taking the necessary actions, regardless of how I felt. When it was time to exercise, I had to exercise. When it was time to practice, I had to practice. When it was time to do anything that was going to move me a step closer to getting out of the wheelchair, I had to do it, no excuses. I would remind myself that I tell my body what to do, and not the alternative. I learned that I had control over my mind and body, and consequently I adopted a do it anyway attitude that pushed me closer to my goals.

Doing it anyway breaks the habit of laziness. It discontinues the use of excuses. It disallows one to be controlled by feelings. It strengthens your internal muscles. It is a step towards controlling your mind, body, and emotions, which dictate your ultimate activity. This is important because your activity determines the results you produce. There should never be a time where the body is dictating the results of your life. Your mind is your greatest asset. It is the central processing system of your body. It is the center of creativity and should therefore control the body. Doing it anyway will create productive habits and internalize new behaviors and activities that consistently move you towards your goal. Doing it anyway assures that the required task is completed. Reaching success requires action. In order to experience success, we must not allow feelings and emotions like being tired and frustrated to control our physical output and direction.

Upon my dismissal from the hospital, my family and I had to adjust. Nothing came easy, but we all went on living a life as best as we knew how. Not much changed in reference to my condition. However, my family was beginning to feel worn down by all of the care and attention I required.

One day, a few months after I was dismissed from the hospital, we were all sitting down having dinner as a family. Mom had prepared a delicious meal that included fried chicken, rice and gravy, and vegetables from the local market. As we all sat at the table enjoying the meal and each other's company, I used the adaptive fork in order to feed myself the rice and vegetables. However, I did not have the dexterity in my hands to pick up a piece of chicken. My mom was kind enough to feed me the chicken. After about 4 to 5 bites, she asked me if the chicken was good. I replied, "Yes, it is delicious!" As I was graciously chewing the chicken she had so kindly given me, she asked if I wanted more. Again I replied, "Yes," to which she replied, "Okay, then you have to get the rest yourself." She put the piece of chicken back on my plate, and removed herself from the kitchen table.

Stunned by the sudden move she had just made, I stared at her as she walked away. I could not understand why she would treat me that way. Feeling betrayed and helpless, I asked her for help. However, she refused to come to my rescue and demanded that I do it myself. I asked my father and sister for help. She then demanded that they not help me and that I do it myself. It made me feel as helpless as ever. I understood that she was trying to help me regain my independence, but I thought I was doing great because I was able to use the splint and adaptive fork. However, that was not enough for her. She did not like to see me that way. Knowing that there was no cure for my spinal injury, she knew I was going to have to relearn a lot of the small stuff, including feeding myself.

So very reluctantly, I began stabbing at the piece of chicken with my fork. Due to the lack of grip and dexterity in my hands, I was unable to grip the chicken. In some instances, I would stab the chicken, but not deep enough for it to remain on the fork until I got into my mouth. I struggled miserably to eat this piece of chicken. My family watched me as I struggled, and encouraged me to keep trying. My dad was saying things like, "Your favorite show is about to go off television, better hurry and finish or you are going to miss it." An hour had gone by and more of the chicken had made it on my shirt, pants, and the kitchen floor than in my mouth. I wanted another piece of chicken because I had only enjoyed the few bites my mother had given me in the beginning. As my mother got up from the sofa to grant my wish, I hoped that she would feed it to me as well so the misery and struggle would come to an end. However, the saga continued as she placed the luscious piece of chicken on my plate and returned to her comfortable spot on the couch. Feelings of defeat and anger were visible on my face. Even though I was embarrassed, I continued to feed myself the chicken. Eventually I ate until I was full.

Day after day, and meal after meal, I went through the process of feeding myself without the assistance of anyone else. My mother demanded that no one help me when I was at the kitchen table. It didn't matter how long it took or how bad it looked, if I wanted to eat, I had to feed myself. That was the bottom line, no questions asked. For about two weeks I cussed and fussed until things started to get easier. I started figuring things out pretty quickly after realizing no one was going to come to my rescue. I began to develop different techniques and strategies that would allow me to get food on the fork and into my mouth. After a while, I had clearly gotten better—a lot better. Most of the food on my plate made it into my mouth instead of on my clothes and on the floor. Although predominantly right-handed, my left hand became more useful when eating. In fact, both of my arms and hands had increased in strength and dexterity as a result of doing it anyway.

Gaining independence offered me a great sense of accomplishment. As I endeavored to accomplish all of my goals, such as pushing a manual wheelchair and walking independently, I vowed to do what was needed, regardless of how I felt physically or emotionally. I was so motivated and excited about reaching my goal, and experiencing the joy it would bring to my life. I knew that God was on my side and if I applied the effort, I would experience the life I imagined: A life free from the shackles of a wheelchair.

I apply the same principles to my life today. I have a daily workout regimen that awakes me at 5 AM every morning with an hour and a half workout prior to going to work. I discipline myself and habitually eat in a manner that will allow my body to perform at its optimal level, and prevent feelings of tiredness and frustration. Ultimately, I have vowed to strengthen not only my body, but also my mind in order to control my emotions and prevent my feelings from controlling me and dictating what actions I take. I am motivated to stick with my regiment because I know what it's like to not have the ability to function at all. The following passage by Raymond Holliwell, and my battle with paralysis, are my driving forces to continue pushing and executing the necessary activities in order to remain successful and walking upright.

As Raymond Holliwell said, "God intended every individual to succeed. It is God's purpose that man should become great. It is God's will that man should not only use, but enjoy, every good in the universe . . . Man is made for progress. Every man contains within himself the capacity for in this development. Advancement into all things is the laws greatest purpose . . . Infinite resources are at man's disposal. There are no limits to his possibilities. He focuses and individualizes the elements, forces, and principles of the whole world. He can develop a wonderful intelligence; thus, all life's questions may be answered, all nature's secrets discovered, and all human problems solved. Nothing is impossible." (Holliwell, 2004)

When you are feeling tired, or fatigued, don't simply go to sleep. It prolongs the process and makes your journey to success even longer. When you give up, you allow your feelings and emotions to defeat and control you. Do not allow the feeling of being tired or frustrated cause you to lose out on the life you imagine. With dedication and persistence, you can create healthy and productive habits to replace the ones that perpetuate the same old bad behavior and procrastination. Procrastination has been said to be the reason that most people fail. In fact, Wayne Gretzky states that "Procrastination is one of the most common and deadliest of diseases and its toll on success and happiness is heavy." Don't let being tired weigh you down. Adopt a do it anyway attitude and go after your dreams with enthusiasm and unwavering effort. Allow yourself time to rest and rejuvenate when necessary, but get back up and make a commitment to achieving your goals, no matter what.

Chapter 10

Fire and Desire: You Got to Want it so Bad You Can Feel it

To desire is to want or wish for something. The fire in your desire is the level of feeling you have towards whatever it is that you desire. In other words, the fire is your emotional attachment to your goals. If you have an intense emotional connection to the thing you desire, it symbolizes an intense burning fire towards its attainment. Should you have a weak emotional attachment to the thing you desire, it symbolizes a small burning fire towards its attainment. According to Napoleon Hill, "The starting point of all achievement is desire." So, in order to reach our goals, we first must have fire and desire.

Hill also states, "Before success comes in any man's life, he is sure to meet with much temporary defeat, and, perhaps, some failure. When defeat overtakes a man, the easiest and most logical thing to do is to quit. That's exactly what the majority of men do." However, when your desire has enough fire behind it, you will never quit and will continue to persistently pursue that which you desire. Many men have traveled the path towards success, but have failed to reach the destination due to an extinguished fire. High levels of success require determination, will, and faith packaged tightly and aimed at the target of success. With enough firepower, this package leaves a blazing trail of accomplishments and achievements along the way. Picture desire as your rocket—the fire beneath your rocket drives you closer and closer to the moon and stars of success.

I've wanted to give up and quit on many occasions. However, my desire to walk again and to be successful was so strong that it would not allow me to stop. Even though my recovery was slow, and difficult, it was my burning desire that kept me going. My desire for success is the reason why I got out of bed when I didn't want to. It drove me to create strategies and routines that would assist my recovery. It was the reason why I forced myself to stay up late and wake up early to work, study, and learn what I needed to do in order to win the battle against paralysis.

It was my burning desire that would not allow me to stop. I studied food that aided in the development and maintenance of the nervous system. I became an expert on health and recovery. I became a dedicated fitness lover. I would stop at nothing to reach my goal. My desire to walk again burned day and night. I wanted success more than I wanted anything else. Frustration and defeat would come and knock me down, but for only a little while. Within a short amount of time I would regroup and reset my focus on my desire. My burning desire kept me level headed, emotionally stable, and grounded in the truth that I was going to win the game of life.

To increase your inner burn, you must recognize the energy of desire as a powerful motivator and creative force. You must state and then focus your desires clearly, and daily, with the reward of success in mind. Ask yourself what you really want. Be as clear and exact as possible. Strengthen your emotional attachment to your desire. Relate emotionally to it by visualizing yourself with it, as it, or while doing it. Imagine what it will feel like driving your new car or taking that exotic vacation. Role-play in your mind and think and feel as you would once you obtain the very thing you desire. For example, imagine the furniture in your brand-new house. How would you set things up? What colors would you use? What type of candles would you burn? What type of smell would you want your visitors to experience? Consistently play this all out in your mind. Do it daily. As a result, you will begin to feel the emotions of having it now.

We are either moving towards something we want, or away from something we don't want. By way of a burning desire, become so determined that you will obtain your goals. Believe with certainty that you will reach your goals. Keep the vision of what you want in front of you, and consistently imagine yourself in possession of it.

Desire, and the energy it creates, affects our intentions and actions. The fire beneath your desire equals your level of determination. It suggests your willingness to take action and remain consistent until the goal is reached. The result of intense fire and desire is success. It is one thing to have a desire for something, but it is a completely different thing to have a burning desire for its attainment.

A burning desire is like a raging flood, stopping at nothing in its path. It cannot be tamed, nor can it be denied. A burning desire is absolutely necessary for high levels of success. Without it, you will not develop the strength, endurance, faith, courage, and mental know-how to overcome temporary defeat. Building a bigger fire under your desire assures you will live a life filled with all that you can imagine. There are no limits to what you can accomplish when fueled by a raging, fire-filled desire.

After a week of living in the critical condition area of the hospital, I was finally moved to a standard hospital room and placed under normal care. The doctors did not share any optimism towards my recovery, even though I asked about it daily. I'd heard miraculous stories of people becoming severely injured and remarkably walking out of the hospital, completely recovered from the injury. Eager to go home and get out of the hospital, I developed the same desire and thought that I could be such a miracle. I wondered what it would take for me to walk out of the hospital. I wondered if I would walk again at all. I wondered what my life was going to be like tomorrow, or in five years, or ten, or twenty. I had established goals and dreams before my injury, but suddenly I didn't know how to go about accomplishing those dreams.

Visits from my family and friends filled my days with laughter, but my nights were full of sleeplessness due to routine nurse interruptions and thoughts of what life was going to be like for me in the future. I missed being with my family and my friends in school. I missed playing football. I heard about how the team won the game after I was carted off the field, and was continuing the remainder of the season without me. I felt like I had been robbed of the thing I loved the most. Although I had the support of my family and friends, I began to get angry. I never envisioned something like this happening to me. Just about every night I would break down and cry, asking the Lord why?

Upon my move from the critical condition unit and settling in the standard hospital room, my physical therapy began. I was scheduled to have therapy twice a day, every day. My therapist would come by my room and perform range of motion activities that involved movement of my arms and legs, back and forth, up and down. As the therapist began to move me, I would experience random involuntary movements of my arm or legs, otherwise known as muscle spasms. At first this was very exciting, as I thought it was part of my recovery, and I was beginning to regain function of my arms and legs. I turned to my therapists and said, "Look! I did it! I can move my leg."

However, my therapists politely informed me that these random involuntary movements were only symptoms of my spinal cord injury. They explained that any type of stimulant, such as muscle stretching or pain that occurs below the level of injury, could trigger a reflex resulting in a muscle spasm. They even implied that I would most likely have the spasms for the remainder of my life. I didn't want to believe what the therapists had said, and refused to accept that the movements were involuntary.

Several times a day I would try to move myself and lift my arms and legs without the assistance of my therapist. It didn't work. I lay in bed devastated by the fact that I could not move my own body. I didn't understand. I was so confused, and was getting increasingly frustrated and irritated. My therapist had to ask me to calm down. I couldn't calm down—I wanted to move my legs and arms freely! A feeling of sadness and emotional pain crept upon me, and I wanted to cry. Tears began to roll down my face. I could tell by my therapist's expression that she could see the pain I experienced. She wanted to help me. She continued on with the stretching and range of motion with my legs and arms. The symptoms of spasms continued as she moved my legs in different positions. It seemed like a hopeless situation, but I refused to believe that this was going to be my condition for the rest of my life. I told myself that I was the one in control, and that I could regain the use of my arms and legs.

My mother and father were also in the room during my scheduled therapy sessions. Upon witnessing all of the muscle spasms I had, they too begin to question why these symptoms were happening. They wanted to know what was causing the spasms. Although we knew we had to face the utter truth, we eagerly awaited some type of good news on which we could hang our hope.

At first we all viewed the muscle spasms as a sign that the nerves I damaged in my accident were awakening. It seemed as though my movement was going to come back after all. The muscle spasms were so intense that they kicked my legs high up from the bed, and they also completely stretched out my arms. However, our hopes that these movements were a sign of recovery were quickly dashed when my doctor confirmed the therapist's report that they were simply side effects of the spinal cord injury.

"After a spinal cord injury occurs," the doctor explained, "the nerve cells below the level of injury become disconnected from the brain at the level, or place, of injury. This is a result of scar tissue forming in the damaged area of the spinal cord, thus preventing messages from below the level of injury from reaching the brain. When a stimulus is applied to the skin in an able-bodied person, a sensory signal is sent to the brain via the spinal cord. The brain then assesses the stimulant, and if the stimulant is thought not to be dangerous, an inhibitory signal is sent down the spinal cord, which cancels the reflex for moving the muscle. In a person with a spinal cord injury, this inhibitory signal is blocked by the structural damage in the spinal cord, and the natural reflex is allowed to continue, resulting in a contraction of the muscle, or muscle spasm."

What the doctor was explaining made sense, but I didn't like hearing it. I didn't like my body moving without me telling it to. Regardless of what I wanted my body to do, or what I was thinking, my body did its own thing. It was as if my body did the very opposite thing that I wanted it to do, and I hated my body for it. I wanted it to end. Threatened by the idea that this could last for the rest of my life, I wanted to know what I needed to do to prevent muscle spasms, or to greatly decrease them. I decided to ask the experts.

The doctor suggested regular stretching and range of motion exercises, but did not offer much more guidance. As a result, I was prescribed baclofen every four hours to keep my muscle spasms in check. This answer was not good enough for me—I had awakened a burning desire within myself to regain control of my body. I demanded more.

For starters, I wanted to work out. I was used to transforming my body into what I wanted it to be. I was a solid football player. I was strong, I was fast, and I was used to a weekly workout regimen. I wanted to apply that same plan of action to this injury and get rid of the paralysis, regain my strength, and prevent further muscle spasms. At least that's what I wanted to do in my mind, but my body prevented me from doing any of that. The only thing I could do was visualize myself working out. Visualize myself lifting my arms and legs. Visualize myself running and lifting weights, and doing all the things I loved to do before my injury. I began to think of things that I could do while lying in the hospital bed, and I started implementing these small stretches and exercises into my daily routine. It was exhausting, but my fire-filled desire for recovery kept me pushing towards my goals.

As Napoleon Hill writes, "What the mind of man can conceive and believe, it can achieve." This maxim is one to live by—and it's evidenced by my recovery. If you want something bad enough to visualize it every day, you will eventually manifest it into your life. If a raging, burning fire fuels your desire for something, you will likely reach your goals because you won't let setbacks or failures keep you from getting up and trying again, and again, until you get what you want. Decide what it is you want for your life, visualize it daily, and create an emotional attachment to the desire so that you can build a fire within yourself that will fuel your journey to success. Get up! Use the fire in your desire to live the life of your dreams.

Chapter 11

WHY? BECAUSE YOU CAN

Life has a tendency to blindside us with unforeseen challenges and crippling situations. Often times the emotional strain, stress and frustration of a particular situation can cause us to ask, "Why?" We find ourselves wondering, "Why is this happening to me? What have I done to deserve this?" We may begin to evaluate ourselves in an effort to find the answer as to why we are deserving of such harsh treatment, or we may try to identify actions or behaviors that would justify the punishment we feel has been cast upon us. I asked myself these questions more a million times throughout the course of my recovery.

Prior to my accident, I was an astounding football player; if it wasn't for my accident, I believe that I could have made it to the pros. After the violent collision and lying motionless on the field, thoughts of never being able to walk crept into my mind. My dream of playing college and professional football was quickly dissipating, only to be replaced with the mental trauma of complete numbness throughout my immovable body. Although I was definitely injured and had certainly damaged my nervous system, my brain hadn't registered that I couldn't move. In my mind, my neurological processing station continued to receive and submit signals as normal, thereby creating a comprehension of what it normally feels like to move and get up.

I could feel my legs and arms move as if I hadn't suffered an injury. I began to question what was wrong and what had happened to me. The thoughts of these unanswered questions combined with the initial feeling of paralysis sent me into a panic. I was fighting frantically to move, but was only able to move my head left to right. I started yelling and screaming fearfully, as the coaches and my mom attempted to calm me down.

The paramedics arrived on the scene and began their trained procedures to stabilize my neck. One of the coaches positioned himself above my head and placed his hands on each side of my helmet in an effort to stabilize my neck. Other coaches and Emergency Medical Technicians (EMTs) grabbed parts of my body, tilted me over on my side, and inserted a flat transport board underneath me. My head, arms, chest, and legs were then strapped down to the board and tightened with fasteners to hold my body still and stable during transport. I was then carried and loaded into the ambulance, which was consistently onsite for all junior varsity and varsity football games. I was transported approximately two miles from Brooks Stadium to South Eastern Regional Hospital.

Upon being rolled into the ER on a hospital bed, I recall the medical staff discussing getting off my gear without causing further injury. It was determined that the best way to remove my gear was to cut it away. The medical staff pulled out these oversized cutters that looked like manual bush clippers and began cutting up the middle of my facemask. They then cut away my shoulder pads and the remainder of my gear.

My parents were not allowed in the emergency room with me at the same time, so they had to take turns standing by my side. It was nice to have one of them in the room with me because their presence brought a level of calmness to the situation. My dad brought about the greatest calmness. Despite the catastrophic situation, he remained calm, leaned over my bed, and smiled at me saying, "It's going to be okay."

The medical evaluation included the American Spinal Injury Association (ASIA) exam, which is used to define and describe the extent and severity of a person's spinal cord injury, as well as to determine future rehabilitation and recovery needs. In most cases the ASIA exam is completed within 72 hours of initial injury, and the person's grade is based on how much sensation he or she can feel at multiple points on the body. The motor exam included testing the five key muscles in each of my arms and legs. The sensory exam involved the light touch and pinprick test, as well as the hot and cold test. However, my injury was so severe that I couldn't distinguish between hot or cold, nor sharp or dull.

As the medical staff was performing the evaluation, I noticed the look on my Dad's face change as he watched the doctors touch and stick me with the sharp edges of the object; he realized my body was not responding. I remember him asking me, "Can you feel that? "I was lying flat on my back and was only able to see the ceiling and things on the left and right side, so I had no idea I was being poked. I responded, "Feel what?" He asked the medical staff to stick me again and looked at me and said, "You can't feel that?" I said, "No, I can't feel anything. What are they doing?" This is when the seriousness of my accident became apparent. We knew at this point that the injury was bad, but witnessing the ASIA evaluation brought a deeper, darker understanding of how threatening this injury was to my body and my future.

The medical staff continued with the evaluation. Not being able to see what they were actually doing to me, I relied on my dad to let me know exactly what was happening. Unable to get a response from parts of my body below my neck, all the way to the bottom of my feet, the medical staff decided to try something different in an effort to determine the severity of my accident. Because there are more nerve endings located in the bottom of the feet, they wanted to see if I could feel pain or any type of sensation in that area. So, they begin cutting the bottom of my feet to see if I could feel it. As they were doing this, the look on my dad's face was horrible. He looked at me and said, "Rodney, you can't feel that? Your feet are bleeding;

they are cutting the bottom of your feet to the point that they are bleeding. You can't feel it?" I responded no and I began to cry. The tears rolled down my face and I just felt so helpless and hopeless. I felt like life was over at that point. I couldn't lift my head to see what was going on, or what they were doing to me, and I couldn't feel anything. I began to ask myself, "Why? Why me? What is it that I have done to deserve this? Why is this happening to me?"

When answering the question, "Why?" the only justifiable answer that I've been able to develop is, "because I have the ability to overcome the challenge that has been placed in front of me." This statement always puts my perspective in check. This statement means that in life, you never know what challenges are going to appear. However, you must understand that whatever the challenge, you have the ability to overcome it. There is no better way to look at a challenge than to ask the question "Why," and then understand that it is because you have the ability to overcome.

Sometimes we look at challenges as problems or roadblocks that slow us down and hinder us from living the life we desire. We view them as obstacles or painful situations that force us to stop moving forward. In most cases, we don't want to stop. We just want to live freely, be unrestricted, and live happily ever after. Challenges are viewed as wrinkles that we must iron out in order to get back to living free. I believe that every challenge that is presented is an opportunity for me, instead of against me. It is an opportunity for me to further develop, grow and create, pushing me closer to success. It is a chance for me to win. Just as force pressed against an orange extracts orange juice, the challenges that press and force more from us, extract the juice within us, thereby exposing our God-given abilities.

Once I understood that my perspective on my accident had a significant impact on the remainder of my life and the possibility of recovery, it changed everything. I could have grumbled and complained for the rest of my life, or wondered why I was the only one attending my own self-inflicted pity party, but I made the decision to view this challenge as an opportunity to bring out the best in myself. I chose to accept the challenge, and as a result, success has been my shadow. As soon as my perspective changed, I knew I could overcome the challenge. So, instead of having a pity party and continuing to ask myself "Why," I started to believe that I could overcome the challenge and began to ask myself "How."

At first I wanted answers from my doctors, my physical therapists, and pills, but as a result of not finding the answers in those areas, I was forced to look within myself. As a result of looking within myself, I became a better person. I realized and developed things within my mind and within my emotions that strengthened my character and broadened my outlook on life. I became more grateful for life itself, and the beauty it brings. I understood the preciousness of life. I understood that life had a very big assignment for me, and life itself was counting on me to complete this task at a satisfactory level. And so, I gathered all my strength and resolve, and put forth the effort necessary to overcome my situation.

It is my belief that this book that you're reading right now is a byproduct of my assignment, and I hope that it is helpful to you. Because not only did I desperately want to walk again, I also severely did not want to fail my assignment. To fail my assignment would be to bury the gift that was given to me by life itself. I felt it would've been like making very poor use of the energy that was granted to me, and the purpose that was assigned to me here on earth. I want to show the world, and my creator, that I was qualified for the assignment given and was completely able to deliver.

Although I have escaped the bounds of the wheelchair and have succeeded in life far beyond what my doctors and many others would have expected, as a result of the traumatizing and debilitating injury I suffered, I still feel that I am on assignment. I'm still faced with daily challenges as a result of this injury. I cannot let my guard down. No, not even for one day. I continuously strive for independence in every level of my life: physical, financial, spiritual, emotional, etc. There are many challenges that I face that must be overcome in order for me to accomplish my task. I believe these challenges will produce the skill, characteristics, and mental acuity necessary for me to meet with success. There's no challenge that can defeat me. I can overcome any challenge and accomplish any goal I choose. I am grateful for my injury and all the effort involved that brought about the awareness that I can do the unthinkable. I believe there are others that embody the "Because you can" philosophy, and I will share their stories with you below.

Art Sanborn lived his entire life on the foundation of biblical scripture. As a missionary in countries like Taiwan and India, Sanborn has seen a multitude of miracles in his travels and mission work around the world. He demonstrated an unwavering faith seen in very few people, which allowed him to overcome some of the most desperate and frightening situations. One of the most terrifying of them all was when a wave slammed him to the ocean floor while surfing in Hawaii, resulting in a broken neck and severe damage to Sanborn's spinal cord. Doctors told Sanborn he would never walk again. However, relying on the power of God, Art did walk again. His far-reaching journey from mission work in an array of countries, to the phenomenon that allowed him to walk again, expresses a life of faith in every circumstance. His life is truly an inspiration that we can overcome any obstacle. (Robins, 2010)

Scott Burrows is living proof that your life can change in an instant. By the age of 19, he was playing college football at Florida State University as a wide receiver. He was also a top-ranked kickboxing champion, with his last fight broadcast by ESPN. On November 3, 1984, Scott was involved in a serious automobile accident that left him paralyzed from the chest down; he was diagnosed as a quadriplegic. However, Scott refused to be sidelined. He made the decision to take action and focus on the positives of the experience, as opposed to dwelling on the negatives. As a result, Scott has committed to live his life by these three principles:

- Vision: You have the power to stretch beyond the self-perceived limitations that have always paralyzed you. Dreaming in Technicolor allows you to expand your resourcefulness and visualize the full measure of your goals.

- Mindset: Face up to what scares you the most. Promise yourself that this time, right now, you'll be more adventurous, more curious and more vulnerable than ever.

- Grit: Relentless determination is the only way to overcome obstacles. Lock in on your goals and don't give up on them until you have reached them.

Scott's application of these three principles has produced astonishing results. Since graduating from college, Scott has formed a successful International Golf Course Development Company, has become a wheelchair athlete, and became a best-selling author with his book, Vision, Mindset, Grit: How to Stand Up When Life Paralyzes You.

Using his paralysis as a visual metaphor, Scott encourages his audiences to stand up to their challenges—regardless of circumstances—using the dynamic principles of Vision, Mindset, and Grit. His presentations are inspirational, focused, and enthusiastically received. Scott has presented to hundreds of associations and corporations in the U. S. and around the globe. He has also shared the stage with iconic celebrities such as Rudolph Giuliani, Terry Bradshaw, and Neil Armstrong. Through his keynote speeches, books, CDs and DVDs, he positively influences the lives of millions. (Burrows, 2012)

Stephen Hawking is the former Lucasian Professor of Mathematics at the University of Cambridge, and the author of A Brief History of Time, an international bestseller. Now Director of Research at the Department of Applied Mathematics and Theoretical Physics, and Founder of the Centre for Theoretical Cosmology at the University of Cambridge, his other books for the general reader include A Briefer History of Time, The Universe in a Nutshell, and the essay collections "Black Holes" and "Baby Universe." In 1963, Hawking contracted motor neuron disease, and was given two years to live. Despite this prognosis, he went on to Cambridge to become a brilliant researcher and Professorial Fellow at Gonville and Caius College. From 1979 to 2009, he held the post of Lucasian Professor at Cambridge, the same chair held by Isaac Newton in 1663. Professor Hawking has over a dozen honorary degrees and was awarded the CBE in 1982. He is a fellow of the Royal Society and a Member of the US National Academy of Science. Stephen Hawking is regarded as one of the most brilliant theoretical physicists since Einstein, and he has achieved greatness in spite of his condition. (Hawking, Unknown)

Theodore DeReese "Teddy" Pendergrass was a successful American solo R&B/soul singer and songwriter. In 1982, he was severely injured in an auto accident, resulting in his being paralyzed from the chest down. He subsequently founded the Tedd Pendergrass Alliance, a foundation that helps those with spinal cord injuries. After his accident, Pendergrass decided to return to the studio to work on new music and struggled to find a recording deal. Eventually he signed a deal and completed physical therapy, and released "Love Language" in 1984. The album included the pop ballad "Hold Me" featuring a then-unknown Whitney Houston. On July 13, 1985, Pendergrass made an emotional return to the stage at the historic Live Aid concert in Philadelphia in front of a live audience of over 99,000, and an estimated 1.5 Billion television viewers. It was the 35-year-old's first live performance following his 1982 accident. In 1988, Pendergrass scored his first R&B #1 hit in nearly a decade with the song "Joy." A video of the song enjoyed heavy rotation on Black Entertainment Television.

Pendergrass kept recording through the 1990s. One of the singer's final hits was the hip-hop leaning "Believe in Love," released in 1994. In 1996, he starred alongside Stephanie Mills in the touring production of the gospel musical "Your Arms Too Short to Box with God." http://en. Wikipedia. Org/wiki/Teddy_Pendergrass - cite_note-7 In 1998, Pendergrass released his autobiography entitled, *Truly Blessed.* Pendergrass did a concert at the Wiltern Theater in Los Angeles, California on February 14, 2002 entitled "The

Power of Love." The concert became the album "From Teddy, With Love," which was released on the Razor & Tie record label later that year. Pendergrass' "Wake Up Everybody" has been covered by a diverse range of acts from Simply Red to Patti LaBelle, and was chosen by Kenneth "Babyface" Edmonds as a rallying cry to mobilize voters during the 2004 Presidential campaign. In addition, Little Brother, Kanye West, Cam'ron, Twista, Ghostface, Tyrese Gibson, 9th Wonder, DMX and DJ Green Lantern have utilized his works. (Wikipedia, 2014)

Mariam Fatima Paré was born in Kenitra, Morocco. Her father, a Marine Sargent, was stationed in Morocco after the Vietnam War to work at the American Embassy; her mother was from nearby Tangier, Morocco. They moved to the United States when she was very young. Mariam always loved to paint, and her family was aware that she was born an artist. This passion for creating art continued throughout her teenage years, and as an aspiring and talented college-level art student, Mariam dreamed of a career making art. However, Mariam's journey was diverted tragically off-course when, in 1996, at the age of 20 years old, she became the victim of gun violence. A single bullet passed through the door of a car, and struck Mariam in the back of her neck, paralyzing her instantly. Her own hands dropped lifelessly from the steering wheel onto her lap. The gunshot wound resulted in a spinal cord injury at the C5/C7 level. For the rest of her life Mariam would be a quadriplegic; permanently unable to walk and with significant loss of function in her upper extremities.

Mariam embarked on a long period of rehabilitation; months and years of slowly and painfully relearning to do everyday activities she had previously taken for granted. She learned to get around using a wheelchair. She learned new ways of holding things with her fingers. She learned to use her mouth for tasks that required a tight grip or precision in her movements. At the Rehabilitation Institute of Chicago, a therapist taught Mariam to hold a pencil in her mouth to write her name. This single lesson exposed Mariam to a new possible way of painting. If she could control a pencil in this way, then why not a paintbrush? With earnest determination, she soon began teaching herself how to paint using her mouth.

In the beginning, the new method of holding the brushes in her mouth to paint was extremely humbling for Mariam. She struggled to paint as well as she once had with her hands. She started slowly with stick figures, even though just months before her injury, she was capable of realistic figure drawing and sophisticated portraits. But she felt all the knowledge was still inside of her, wanting and waiting to be expressed. To Mariam, after feeling the full weight of her limitations that first year with paralysis, it felt like a miracle that she still had the ability to do the one thing she loved most - to paint - even if it was in a new and unusual way. The gratitude and joy she felt from re-establishing that ability pushed her onward and gave her hope in the midst of an otherwise uncertain future.

She began to practice painting by mouth every day. Through a combination of sheer will and family support, Mariam carved out a meaningful life after her injury. She broadened the idea of what she thought was possible for herself and continued to develop as an artist and "mouth painter." In 2003, she began a degree in Fine Art and finished an Associates Degree in Graphic Design, and another in Web Design. In 2006, Mariam was accepted as a member of the Association of Mouth and Foot Painting Artists (MFPA), an international, exclusive, and esteemed association of artists who paint professionally either by use of their mouth or feet. Mariam also licenses her mouth-painted art internationally in the form of greeting cards, calendars and other products. Since 2010, Mariam has been a member of the Associate Board of the Rehabilitation Institute of Chicago, where she helps to coordinate art exhibits to raise funds for RIC's art therapy program, as well as to promote awareness about the benefits of art therapy.

Mariam has provided inspirational and memorable speaking services for many groups and companies such as The Million Dollar Round Table, The Rehabilitation Institute of Chicago, Illinois Spinal Cord

Injury Group, the MFPA, Spinalpedia. Com, and more. Seventeen years after her violent injury, painting by mouth has become second nature for Mariam, who now proudly possesses painting skills tantamount to that of any able-bodied counterpart.

The people mentioned above, myself included, made a choice: A choice to overcome the tragedy that was bestowed upon us. We all had every right to throw in the towel and allow tragedy to overtake us. We all had a long, demoralizing and daunting road to emotional recovery, which required a level of strength and faith rarely discovered. However, despite it all, we believed in our inner ability to overcome. We consistently, day-after-day-after-day, made the decision to believe, focus, and pursue what was innately possible, in lieu of focusing on the impossible. We all developed the "I Can" attitude.

Sometimes tragedy strikes and knocks us down, and often times it seems impossible to get up. What is key during these moments is how we respond when tragedy hits. It is very easy to let go of hope, and start asking the question, "Why?" Instead of giving in to this despair, we must realize that we can overcome any obstacle put on our path. We must realize what we are capable of, and focus on success. When we do this, our perspective of tragedy will shift, and allow us to travel a path to victory and success. The next time you ask yourself, "Why?" Answer, "Because I can!"

Chapter 12

Your Purpose is Not to Set the Example, but to Be the Example

As I battled my injury, there were times when I felt very alone. I did not have any friends who had experienced similar trauma. I wanted someone that I could reach out and touch, someone who was a real live example of how to overcome such a debilitating and traumatizing injury. I needed the inspiration. While I was thankful to Dennis Byrd for his example of overcoming a spinal cord injury, however I didn't have him there in arms reach for support. There was no one that I could sit down with and ask, "What should I do now?" What is my next step?"

As I looked around at the people in my life experiencing their own challenges, I realized that they too were looking for a sense of inspiration and seeking answers to their questions of how to overcome adversity. As a result of being determined to overcome my own injury, I noticed that I began to be the inspiration that people needed to see. So, I placed the responsibility on my shoulders and set out to do whatever was necessary to overcome and provide examples for others to follow. It seemed as though in every hospital facility that I visited, and every physical therapy institution to which I was admitted, I became the focal point of attention as a result of my attitude and determination towards defeating my injury. I got the feeling that those other patients facing a similar challenge just accepted their situation. Yes, they attended physical therapy, and did the things the doctors requested that they do, but I didn't sense they had the fire or the desire to put their injuries to sleep. Their pervasive attitude was, "If I recover, that's great. If not, I will learn to live with what I have." Whereas my attitude was, "There is no other option other than to defeat the injury, and to regain my life. I will stop at nothing to regain what has been taken from me."

It was my philosophy that a high level of determination and a positive attitude were absolutely necessary to overcome an injury that robs you of your physical ability and threatens your emotional and mental stability. I hated to see people suffer from such debilitating injuries; so, every chance I got, I wanted to show others who were in a similar condition that they could still win the game of life, despite their injury or disability. As a matter of fact, with the right attitude, we all can recover from injury, no matter how debilitating and traumatizing it may be. I was determined and excited to share my philosophy to the world.

People are more responsive to people they can interact with in person. It means so much more when you can actually have a conversation with the person who has done something tremendous, or who aligns with your own personal goals or personal situation. Yes, is great to have examples that you can go back, take a look at, and implement in hopes of reaching the same success; however, it means so much more and has a much greater benefit when you can see the person with your own eyes and perhaps reach out to them. Being an example allows you to be more personal, and to be the person who takes the time to interact with others and share stories of success. Being an example allows you to step outside of the box and be the person who does not allow the challenge to overcome him, but who is actually overcoming the challenge himself. When you are an example, you can actually stand up a say "I did it" to the world.

I consider myself an example of grit, determination, longevity, endurance, and toughness; I am the epitome of mental strength. I remember so vividly being admitted over the course of a summer for intense physical therapy at the Cape Fear Valley Regional Medical Center in Fayetteville, North Carolina. My purpose there was to undergo intense physical therapy in hopes of learning how to better control my gait and advance my feet forward during walking attempts. There was a particular guy there, Mr. Rico, who had suffered a gun wound that left him paralyzed from the neck down. Miraculous as it was, Mr. Rico had experienced a great amount of recovery, as initially he was not even able to breathe on his own, talk, or perform activities necessary for independent daily living. Despite these advancements, Mr. Rico had a very grim outlook on life. He thought life was over for him, and that there was no reason for him to put forth any effort in physical therapy because he had no hope of recovering. It saddened me to see Mr. Rico in this state.

My daily regimen included intense physical training, and multiple attempts to stand and walk, which I looked forward to daily. I was beyond happy to be able to receive training and assistance with standing and walking twice a day. During this time, I was completely focused on regaining my strength, and possibly learning how to independently walk. My attitude was very optimistic towards my goals and I was focused on them like a laser. As a result of my attitude towards my recovery, it was suggested that I talk with Mr. Rico in hopes of motivating him to complete his physical therapy and re-learn how to perform daily activities on his own. As with all patients seen by the physical therapy staff at the rehab center, the goal was for all of us to become as independent as possible. Mr. Rico and I became best friends while in rehab. Not only did Mr. Rico become motivated to complete his physical therapy and independently take care of himself, he also regained his strength to walk and perform his activities of daily living. To this day, Mr. Rico is alive, well, and walking upright. He attests the turning point in his life and the shift in his mindset to a few key discussions we had during the early moments of our relationship. There are countless other experiences that I've had where I was able to inspire others with my attitude towards my recovery. Not only have I affected people who have suffered a similar accident or injury, but also able-bodied people have provided their feedback as to how the determination that I display helped them to overcome many challenges and situations they've experienced in their lives. I had some people tell me how they used to complain about simple things in life, but when they saw what I went through, the attitude I displayed towards it, and the determination that I had to overcome it, they don't complain anymore. Many people have changed their perspective on life and how they view their challenges because of me. I am truly blessed and grateful to be able to positively influence people's lives.

Throughout my very short football career, I was considered a star with a bright future. My family and all those around me treated me as though they knew I would excel to a high level in football. We were all excited and anxious for what the future held. It seemed I was headed into the limelight, and we were all ready to live it up. There were many discussions about what we were going to do once I made it. We all had a dream, and I was the guy that was going to make it happen for everyone, for my entire family. As a result, I had a close relationship with not only my immediate family, but also with many of the cousins I grew up with in my younger days. As I was approaching the age where I was allowed to hang out more with my friends and go to parties, there was much anticipation of what that life was going to be like. I was eager to live it.

However, on the day of my injury, as I was pushed out of the emergency room headed towards the ambulance that would take me to the helipad to be transferred from Southeastern Regional Hospital to Duke University Medical Center, to my surprise, I was greeted by my cousins and family members who were coming to celebrate one of my cousin's birthday and my very first win of the season. Excited and flattered to hear the news, I wished that I could get up and go and be a part of the party. Yet, I knew in my mind that there was no cure for spinal injury. I wondered whether I would ever be able to get up and recover from this accident. I knew that most paralyzed people remain that way for the rest of their lives. I did not want that person to be me. I never thought that I would experience something so devastating.

As we approached Duke University Medical Center, I could hear the engine of the chopper downshift and I knew we were soon to land. Upon de-boarding the helicopter, I was greeted by my grandfather who immediately began offering his sympathy. His first words when he saw me were, "It's going to be okay grandson, it's going to be okay." Not knowing the extent of my injury, only what was given to him over the phone from my parents, I knew he was being strong for me and I needed it. It was a two-hour drive from Lumberton to Duke University Medical Center, so I knew it would be a little while before I saw my mother and father; my grandfather was all that I had until they arrived. I was fortunate my grandfather lived in Durham, North Carolina and was able to accompany me to the hospital. As I was rushed into the emergency room, the medical staff began their evaluation of the severity my accident. At this time all I wanted to do was sleep. But they would not allow me to do so. Their reasoning behind not allowing me to sleep was that my body was under a lot trauma, and going to sleep could cause me to go into shock.

During the evaluation, the medical staff informed me that they needed to pump my stomach. In order to do this they had to insert a tube in my mouth and down through my esophagus to my stomach. As the staff began to insert the tube in my mouth, they reminded me to continuously swallow. It was supposed to make the process easier, however it made me feel like I wanted to vomit. The purpose of pumping my stomach was to get rid of any fluids because being immobile made it easy for liquids in my body to become stagnant and cause sickness. I learned that when you are paralyzed, sicknesses like the flu and pneumonia are great threats to the body.

In an effort to keep the fluids in my lungs moving and to prevent pressure sores, the doctors placed me on what is now called an EPOS-bed, a special hospital bed with an automatic positioning system that allows the repositioning of patients with limited mobility. The effects of the injury severely weakened my respiratory system, and as a result I couldn't inhale or breathe as strongly as I used to. This was a major threat to my health. Not being able to fully expand my lungs prevented the separation of mucus and other liquids. If this doesn't happen regularly, you could develop pneumonia. By lying on the rotating bed, it allowed the fluids in my body to move and not remain stagnant, thus preventing pneumonia. Because the bed rotated from one side to the other, I never remained in one position too long, which also helped to prevent skin breakdown and body sores. I remember feeling imprisoned after being placed on the rotating bed. As if being paralyzed wasn't horrible enough, being strapped to this bed made me feel like I had committed a crime and was a threat to society. I say that jokingly, but I was strapped to the bed as if I was a convict and no one wanted me to escape. I had a strap around my chest, around my waist, and around each of my arms and my legs. I know it was necessary because the bed rotated from left to right, and the straps prevented me from falling out of the bed, but it was the most uncomfortable, mentally straining and debilitating contraption I had ever experienced. As I lay on the hospital bed, I knew my days of playing football were over. Not only did I feel like I had let myself down, but I also felt like I had let my family down. I was the guy that was going to make it; I was going to set the example for my family. My goal was to change our lives while doing something that I loved.

Today, as I look back on my experiences, I realize there was a greater purpose for my life. I've gained so much motivation and encouragement from giving others hope and inspiration to keep going. There are not many people who overcome the bounds of a spinal cord injury. More have succumbed to the grips of spinal injury than those who have succeeded—But I vow to change that. My motivation to succeed is not only to regain the independence and functionality I once had, but also to encourage those who may have suffered a similar injury or who have experienced any type of debilitating challenge. I want to be an example of how to overcome the grips of obstacles and temporary defeat. I want to show others how to stand up and rise above with all their might and intensity in an effort to overcome. I want to be a beacon of hope, a guiding light.

There were several individuals whom were my beacon of hope and a guiding light in my time of need. Whenever things seemed dark and unbearable, I turned to my mother for her aggressiveness and determination. If there was ever something that she wanted to do, she did it. She let me know that I was going to have to fight for every inch of recovery just as I fought for every yard on the field. My dad and others such as, Mr. Breeden, and Dr. Washington served as examples of absolute poise in the face of adversity. No matter what the challenge, they did not lose control of their emotions. They remained strong. They always seemed to have a good attitude, and were smiling no matter what was going on in their lives. They were powerful examples for me during my recovery. They helped turn things around for me after my injury, and placed me on a path towards being an example for others. Dr. Washington always had an attitude of "let go and let God." She advised that it really didn't matter why the accident happened. The objective now was to overcome it and be an example to others.

An important aspect of overcoming adversity is to believe that you will succeed. You should always have a positive outlook and attitude towards overcoming your challenges. When you radiate this type of positivity and hope, others will be inspired. When you become an example, you can help others recover and reclaim their own lives. When you support others along their journey, it also helps to strengthen your own resolve. Live your life as an example for others, and you will improve many lives, including your own.

Chapter 13

YOUR MIND IS YOUR GREATEST ASSET

When facing a major challenge, the battle is won or lost in the mind. In some cases, we defeat ourselves as a result of fear, indecisiveness, or a negative outlook. Regardless of what you may be currently experiencing, where you are now and where you want to go are directly related to the perception you have of yourself and your belief of it actually happening. It has less to do with your physical ability, but it does test your mental strength and faith. The mind is key for accomplishing goals and defeating challenges. You will sabotage your chances of being successful if you don't have the right mindset. Negative thinking begets negative results, just as positive thinking begets positive results. You could have great athletic ability, but if you do not possess the proper mindset in which to channel your athletic ability, it will not bring you much value. The single most important key to overcoming any challenge or seeking success is the mindset you have towards defeating it, or obtaining it.

I almost died out there on the field. No, my life was not at risk of being lost, but my mental and emotional states were certainly at risk of never ever being the same. There were many times when I felt that the mental and emotional strains were just too unbearable for me. I didn't know how to deal with the anger. The fact that I could potentially be in a wheelchair for the rest of my life was overwhelming. I felt like I had no reason to live. It was as if I had no self-worth. I felt like I was of no value to myself, let alone anyone else. It felt as though no one would ever want me or need me. I went from being the center of attention in my family to feeling like I was a burden. As a result of all of the care that I needed, I felt like I actually devalued my family. I did not want to live. This was not how I envisioned myself and I hated every second and moment that I remained in that state. The fact that there was no cure and nothing the doctors could do to change my condition made me feel hopeless and powerless. I had no way of changing, and I had no way of controlling it. It was controlling me.

I remember expressing how I felt about the situation to my mother. One day while she was helping me get dressed, I began to tell her how much I hated my life after the accident. I admitted how much it hurt to feel like I had let her down. I expressed how I wanted to raise a family and bring grandchildren over for Sunday dinner. I told her how I didn't know I was going to do that now. I didn't know how I was going to raise a family. I felt like no one was going to want me. Therefore, I would never get married and have kids. I didn't know if I could even have kids. How was I going to make money? Who was going to hire me? What type of work could I do? Her response to me was, "Your body may be injured, but son there's nothing wrong with your mind. If you put your mind to it you can do anything. You only have to figure it out." Her statement resonated with me and changed my perception of who I was. I began to look at myself as if nothing was wrong with me because she was right—my mind wasn't injured at all. I was the same person mentally as I was before I got hurt. I realized that although my body was injured, my mind was perfect.

As I thought about her response, I began to realize that I still had use and full capacity of the most important asset of my body: my mind. I was excited about it because I felt like it was my way out. As I began to understand and study the power of the mind, I realized that I could defeat my injury through thought. I began to view this experience in my life as a challenge instead of as a defeat. I embraced it as an opportunity to overcome. I believed that if I thought about it hard enough and long enough, I could possibly come up with a means to defeat the injury and walk again. So, I began to find out more about myself. I began to study self-development and I began to understand that the real power that I possess lies within my mind. I came to the understanding that I am a spiritual being with an intellect that lives inside the body. Most importantly, I realized that the body is an instrument of the mind. I began to pick and choose what to get emotional about. I focused all my energy and emotion and desire towards recovery and dismissed the emotions of fear, defeat, lack, and negativity. I developed a positive outlook on life and focused on what I wanted—my goals, my dreams, my desires and I began to think about how I could accomplish those things: What could I do to make them happen?

As a result of this exploration, ideas, concepts, and strategies, plans began to surface in my mind and I immediately acted upon them. For example, I would imagine myself driving a car even though I didn't have the physical ability to drive the car. I just knew I wanted to drive the car, so I kept imagining driving the car that I wanted. I kept imagining walking. I would imagine myself walking so much that I had dreams about walking everywhere that I went. Even though I didn't know how I would, I began to believe and have faith that I was going to walk again. I believed that I was going to accomplish my dreams and desires.

From a fundamental point of view, having a clear picture and order of what you intend to accomplish in your mind is the first step towards its attainment. Many famous works of literature, and great writers, agree that the mind is our greatest asset. Napoleon Hill says, "Man can create nothing which he does not first conceive in the form of an impulse of thought." (Hill, 2009, p. 295) Likewise, as is written in the Bible, "As a man thinketh, so is he." (Proverbs 23:7) Believe it or not, you are what you think about. In other words, you and the things in your environment are a result of the things that you've been thinking about in the past. As Earl Nightingdale put it, "You become what you think about." In order to change your current environment, you must first change your thoughts. The thoughts you choose will ultimately, and eventually, determine the results you experience in your life.

As you change your thoughts and continually impress the new thoughts into your subconscious mind, they become part of the new you and your new personality will begin to express itself through new actions. As a result of new actions, you begin to experience new results. Again, I turn to Napoleon Hill who wisely says, "Man's thought impulses begin immediately to translate themselves into their physical equivalent, whether those thoughts are voluntary or involuntary." (Hill, 2009, p. 328)Why let negative thoughts determine your life? Take control of your mind, and live the life of your dreams.

Upon being dismissed from the hospital and returning home to my family, and before that pivotal conversation with my mother, I was mad at the world for the injury I suffered. I hated every moment of being in a wheelchair, and I equally hated the fact that I had to be cared for and waited on hand and foot for anything and everything that I needed. I felt angry: Angry at the world, and angry with everyone around me. I was mad. My nights and days were spent in fear and anger at the fact that I suffered such a freak accident. There was no malfunction; my form was perfect when I made the tackle. At night I would look back at my life, the short 15 years I had lived, and remember how active I was. I would reminisce on how I used to drag a lawnmower through my neighborhood and ask neighbors if they would like for me to mow their lawn, and how I made sure my mom and dad's car was always clean, and how I was proud to present them with a clean car at least twice a week, weather permitting. I reminisced on working out with my buddies in the gym, and how I became so obsessed with working out that I rearranged my dad's barn so that I could set up my own personal home gym. Most of all I reminisced on the camaraderie amongst my teammates and all the fun times we shared on and off the field. Reminiscing on the past and feeling the reality of not being able to do those things anymore brought about anger, fear, and at times a bad attitude towards others and life. It stole my motivation and prevented me from progressing forward. My emotions were uncontrollable and often times I would negatively express myself and slander my family members who were only attempting to help me through providing the best care possible.

Among all of the anger and negativity I expressed, I did not gain anything in return. It actually made my situation worse. As a result of my anger and miserable attitude, I made little progress towards living life. It wasn't until I changed my perception of my injury and my attitude towards life that things began to move towards goodness. Once I began to be thankful for life itself and the ability I had despite my injury, I was able to focus on what I could do to better my situation. I began to search for ways to accomplish my desires with or without a disability. I believed that if I could win in my mind, then I could win in my environment. So I wanted to do all I could do to ensure my success as an individual. It didn't matter if it meant I had to work harder than the average person, my mind was made up to do whatever it took to succeed.

I knew I couldn't compete with my fellow brethren physically for a job, so I made sure to make myself either equally or more qualified on paper for the positions I was seeking. I made a commitment to do all of the things I describe in this book. The following four key principles were the axioms of my success:

1. Demanding more from myself than anyone else

2. Being willing to do whatever it takes

3. Defeating moments of despair with planned action and certainty

4. Consulting with a mentor

To strengthen my mind during my journey, I became a student of self-development. One of the greatest benefits was the keen understanding that I was created in the image and likeness of God. We all possess the same characteristics of the architecture of the universe. This revelation brought about a sense of awareness within my life, one that I wanted to maintain and protect. I made up my mind that I solely was responsible for all that existed in my life and if anything needed to be changed, I was the one responsible for changing it. I came to the realization that I was the only problem I would ever have, which also meant that I was the solution. Therefore, I made it a habit to evaluate myself often. Realizing my thoughts were connected to my feelings allowed me to change the tune whenever negativity invaded my mind. I would ask myself, "Are my current thoughts serving me? Are they bringing value to my current situation, or are they perpetuating the experience?" I would ask the same questions relative to my daily actions in order to ensure I was staying on track, and appropriately implementing my plan. This was very difficult at first, but I kept doing it. As a result, I found I began to feel better emotionally. It takes a lot of energy to be mad and angry all day. My outlook on life began to change, and I became motivated to live. I discovered power and energy within myself, and I began to believe in the incredible.

I began to believe that I could do what many thought was impossible. I surrounded myself with people who believed in me and were willing to provide their support. Most important, I held on to my dream, and refused to let it go until it was attained. According to Napoleon Hill, "Mind control is the result of self-discipline and habit. You either control your mind or it controls you. There is no halfway compromise. The most practical of all methods for controlling the mind is the habit of keeping it busy with a definite purpose, backed by a definite plan. Study the record of any man who achieves noteworthy success, and you will observe that he has control over his own mind, moreover, that he exercises that control and directs it toward the attainment of definite objectives. Without this control, success is not possible." (Hill, 2009, p. 366)Your mind is truly your greatest asset, so appreciate it and use it to add value to your life.

Chapter 14

Take Responsibility to Change the Situation

Let's be honest; most of us complain about the way things are going in our lives. This is especially true when we fall short of what we desire. It's all too easy to point the finger or blame external circumstances for our life failures. However, if change is what we seek, we must take responsibility for our own predicaments and results. Things happen in life beyond our control, and there's no way of getting around that; however, it is still our responsibility to ensure our lives turn out the way we want. We must be willing to step up to the plate and adjust when life throws a curve ball. We can't blame anyone or anything else. We have to determine what adjustments need to be made, and then take action. There's no value in complaining and expressing frustration when things don't turn out the way you expected. If you don't like a particular situation, then change it. Take the responsibility to do something about it and make the situation better. Bickering and complaining offers no return on your time investment. As a matter of fact, the more you bicker and complain, the worse you are going to feel, and as a result you get stuck in a vicious cycle of negativity. Stop complaining and accept things for what they are—then with a smile, do all you can to make things better.

When I was paralyzed, taking responsibility meant accepting the fact that, just like my injury, things happen in life that are beyond my control. Whether good, bad, or neutral, this applies to all situations. As stated earlier, we often blame others or circumstances for the problems or challenges we experience. Sometimes we take out our frustration on those around us; I know because for a time that is exactly what I did. I blamed the world because I was mad at the world and everybody in it.

At the time of my accident, I was playing football, and wasn't doing anything wrong to warrant such a terrible life-long punishment. I felt like I didn't deserve the injury or the pain and suffering that went along with it. I felt sorry for myself, and I felt bad that my family had to take care of me. It felt like there was no point in living. What did I have to offer? What value was I to anyone? And besides, I couldn't live the life I wanted to live. There was no cure for a catastrophic spinal cord injury. It didn't seem like things were going to get better. The doctors didn't have any answers for me. So I was just mad at everything in my life. Mad at everything that I had to go through.

I felt like I had been betrayed. I loved the game of football and it was taken away from me. I felt like life was unfair. I couldn't be a typical 15-year-old kid anymore. As a matter of fact, the repercussions of the accident were going to follow me for the rest of my life, and as a result, I felt that life had hit me with a low blow. No one should have to deal with such a tragic situation, but especially not a teenager. I had to think about everything differently and strategically; and I was not happy about it. I hated every minute of it. I went to sleep mad and woke up mad. It was bad enough that the doctors told me that I would never walk again, but I just couldn't handle the reality and the emotional stress and pain of not being able to get up and move my body whenever I wanted to.

As an individual and a football player, I carried a lot of confidence and kicked around a boatload of testosterone out on the field; however, after the accident, my ego was crushed and I felt like nothing. My days were filled with plenty of self-pity and as a result my attitude towards everyone and everything was infectiously sour. After about a year of cussing and fussing with my family, I finally came to the realization that my nasty attitude and tainted outlook on life were not going to get me anywhere. I knew I had to get a grip on my situation and myself if I was going to find happiness and peace of mind.

I could have identified 100 reasons why this should not have happened to me, and thousands of excuses to continue to feel sorry for myself, but the truth of the matter is that it did happen and I had to deal. No one was experiencing what I was experiencing. They didn't feel the pain and they didn't feel the agony, so I had every right to have an attitude and to curse and express my frustration. However, I had to take responsibility for what had occurred in my life. It didn't matter whether the accident was a result of right or wrongdoing. All that mattered was my current situation, and what I was going to do in order to better the situation for tomorrow. I had to get out of the blame game, and I had to stop feeling sorry for myself.

I recognized that sometimes in life you are thrown challenges and situations that are difficult. However, life goes on. I had to accept my accident and my life after the accident. It didn't kill me, so I had to keep going and keep living, and I needed to make the best of my life and what was left of it. I knew that I was the only person who was responsible for making sure that happened, so I took the responsibility.

There were several steps I took to change my situation. First, I re-evaluated my current condition and state of mind. After realizing that I had a bad attitude and outlook on life, I was determined to be more optimistic. I became conscious of when my attitude turned sour, and made a commitment to change it by filling up my mind with positive thoughts. I spent more time in church and in prayer, and I began reading stories of people who recovered from debilitating injuries in an attempt to regain hope that I too could overcome. I also changed my outlook on life. I took a look at all of my goals prior to my injury, and refocused on the ones I wanted to pursue despite being in a wheelchair. After I identified all of the goals that I wanted to accomplish, I figured out everything that I needed to do in order to make that happen.

In addition, I changed my perspective on my accident. Instead of looking at it as unfortunate and debilitating, I started looking at it as an opportunity. I began to focus on the possibilities. What would happen if I were to walk again? I focused on how it would feel if I were able to overcome. How many people could I help? What type of opportunities would open up for me if I were to defeat my injury? In asking and answering those questions, my mind began to generate ideas that clarified my injury as more of an opportunity than a challenge. I began to be thankful. I wanted nothing more than to take full advantage of my opportunities.

I started visualizing what life would be like five or ten years down the road if I were to overcome my injury. I thought about things that I would do to live my life to the fullest. This book was an idea I had while sitting in my electric wheelchair and thinking about what life would be like if I overcame the odds. Although it has taken a lot longer than I expected to get to this point, I am so gracious that I finally made it and am able to write this book. At the time of my recovery, I wanted nothing more than to be an example, to defeat my injury, and to be someone that other people could look to for hope and strength. I wanted to show people how to overcome their difficulties and look at their situation as opportunity instead of a tragedy. That became, and still is, my purpose in life.

Despite my debilitating injury, it became my purpose to be as successful as possible and to be an example to people. Often times, people who suffer this type of injury feel worthless and undervalued. A lot of times they don't have anyone to look up to. Often times, people with disabilities are cast aside, and are overlooked and not recognized. People see them as abnormal or insignificant, but I wanted to make sure that I remained significant and I was willing to show the world that despite my injury, I am still here.

Despite where you may be in life, what you may be feeling, or what you have gone through, you have a purpose and you can bring about change to not only those people who are in a similar situation, but to people all over the world who have suffered any type of challenge or difficult experience. The best way to convince others of their worth is to be an example.

Therefore, I redefined my desires and my goals around that purpose, and I set out to accomplish them. I developed a plan of everything that I wanted to achieve. Once I reached one milestone, I celebrated briefly and began immediately working towards the next. I made several mistakes along the way, however I didn't let those mistakes get me down or stop me from reaching my goals. I continued to press on and made adjustments when necessary; most importantly, I remained focused on my desired outcomes. I leaned on the people in life who provided me with support, guidance, and encouragement. I placed my attitude upon the foundation that I was going to make it happen, or die trying. Losing was simply not an option. I closed my mind and emotions to prevent negativity, and only allowed in positivity.

All of my efforts absolutely changed my situation. As a result of taking responsibility, not only did I change my life, but I also helped change the lives of thousands of people. As a matter of fact, I'm still in the process of changing my situation for the better, as well as helping others change their situation for the better. My purpose continues to live on and expand well beyond those who are in my immediate location, reaching individuals around the world. I feel more responsible than ever to continue to reach my goals and provide people with an example of how to succeed in overcoming adversity and enjoying victory.

As I look back at my life, the only thing I would've done differently to change my situation would definitely be to have made the decision that I was going to change a lot sooner than I did. It took about a year for me to get my mind and emotions in a place where I was willing to accept what had happened to me and make a decision to change it. During the time of frustration, agony, and misery, I could have been implementing my strategy for change and could perhaps be a lot further than where I am now. I lost valuable time, and in the process, I hurt people's feelings because of my bad attitude. In addition, I could have probably helped a lot more people than I have up to this point.

Life is precious and short. Every minute of your time is valuable— more valuable than any amount of money. We don't have any time to waste on expressing negative emotions, perpetuating negative energy, and ultimately creating negative results. There's enough negativity in the world without us creating more of it. Therefore, we should use our time wisely and purposefully in order to bring about positive and influential change to our lives and to the lives of others.

There are a number of things you can do to take responsibility and change your current status quo. Begin the healing process by mentally freeing yourself from the shackles of the past. Release the thoughts and things that have cluttered your mind. Get rid of resentment, emotional rehashing, and refighting of past unalterable events. What has happened has happened. Let go of worrying about it. Get rid of guilt, a powerful and negative emotion akin to resentment that forms a negative self-image that prevents you from moving forward. The past is unchangeable, thus guilt is unnecessary. All great achievers have been visionary individuals who projected and focused on the future rather than belaboring over the past. The idea is to focus on what will be rather than what was, and to take action and bring these things into fruition.

I've learned that life is a series of endings and beginnings. We should not reflect back on our lives in anger, nor look forward in fear, but be consciously aware of what surrounds us. Living your life through the images of days gone by will never lead to affective change or worthwhile success. You must take responsibility for your present condition, by making a decision to create a brighter future through pursuing the images of the good you desire. Taking action towards changing your situation offers you the opportunity to experience your dreams. Change your situation by taking the responsibility to look up, look ahead, and form the life you choose to live.

Chapter 15

Defeat Moments of Despair Through Planned Action

It was not easy overcoming my injury. There were many times that I wanted to just give up and die. I had to deal with things like increased muscle tone and muscle spasms, I had to be catheterized multiple times a day, and it seemed like I had to take a pill for every bodily function. It was just downright depressing. Sometimes I couldn't sleep well because of the muscle spasms, which would wake me up throughout the night. When I was able to return to school, I had to have an assistant take notes for me, ensure that I got to class safely, and take care of my catheterization schedule throughout the day. In addition, during this time I wasn't able to feed myself with a regular fork. I had to use an adaptive fork, which made me feel awkward and abnormal compared to all of my other classmates.

Reuniting with my classmates was also very awkward and at times led to depression. A lot of my friends didn't know how to accept me. I could tell most of them weren't used to being around someone in my condition. Quite frankly, I didn't know how to handle my condition. I did the best that I could do each day, but I often felt depressed and lonely. At times, it seemed the only friend I had was my assistant. Before the accident it was me and the boys. It was normal for me to spark up conversations in between classes, as there was always the possibility of running into someone I had not seen in a while, or even meeting someone new. After the accident, my assistant and I left my classes 10 minutes before the bell rang in order to get to my next class and avoid being in the hallways when all the other students were running around. The school decided this was best because I could move around the hallways freely without accidentally hurting anyone with my wheelchair. As a result, I didn't have a whole lot of interaction with my peers other than during classes, in the cafeteria during lunch, or after school in the pickup area. Sometimes I would deliberately wait around for classes to end in order to be in the hallways with all the other students. However, there were other times when I didn't want to be around anyone because I was so depressed. Daily, I fought a battle for survival.

Although my friends were happy to see me back, there was a sense of fear and uneasiness because they didn't want to hurt me in any way. They were also curious about life for me with this injury. Most of the students at school had known me since junior high school. They were used to my very active, friendly and bubbly personality, before the injury. Now they could see the pain, frustration and fear on my face. Although I tried to hide it, it was obvious that I was going through a lot of physical and emotional stress. One day, during a break between classes, a somewhat distant friend of mine came up and welcomed me back to school and provided her sympathy for the tragedy I suffered. She began to question my disability and how things were going since the accident. In an attempt to stay positive, I mentioned that things were good and moving in the right direction. Growing in curiosity, she began to question whether or not I had a girlfriend. As my mind began to ponder the physical restrictions my disability could cause in a relationship with the opposite sex, she reached out her hand and placed it on my thigh. She began sliding her hand back and forth on my thigh while looking directly in my eyes with a look of earnest expectation. While she continuously rubbed her hand softly up and down my leg as I was seated in my wheelchair, she looked at me and asked me, "Can you feel that?" At that very moment, all of the flatter, seduction, attraction, and pleasure of having an attractive girl show an interest in me and actually touch me left my mind, and the feeling of agony and devastation swept in and took over every emotional cell I had in my body. Knowing I would not have been able to feel it if she had a razor blade in her hand cutting my flesh to the very bone, I responded, "Yes, I can feel it." I felt that if she knew that there was no possible way for her to bring me pleasure with touch and sensation, all of the desire and attraction that she had for me would be shattered into pieces.

Upon my response, she pulled her arm back with a sense of accomplishment and gain. The class bell rang, indicating the start of the next period. As we both became eager to get to class, she smiled and said that we would be talking soon. With 1,000,001 things going through my mind about where this would lead, and how things would be relative to my disability, I responded, "Okay I will talk to you soon." She walked away with a sense of confidence. It was almost as if she had identified and established her starting point. As I continued on to class, I could not wait for this school day to end. I was overwhelmed by my emotions. Her question triggered thoughts that I had consistently pushed to the back of my mind. My philosophy was that I would overcome this injury before having to deal with such a devastating situation.

Thoughts were pushed down of what life would be like if I ever decided to establish a relationship, get married, or even have kids. How was I going to have a girlfriend in this condition? I thought that no one was going to want to deal with my disability on a regular basis. Hell, I didn't want to deal with it, so I certainly didn't want to drag someone else into my problems. It was painful enough that my mother and father had to drastically alter their lives in order to make sure that I was cared for.

Immediately following her question, all of these thoughts came to the forefront of my mind—I could no longer push them down. Although I had regained some strength and movement in my legs,

I had not yet regained any sensation. It had taken everything that I had to hold back the tears. I felt like breaking in these moments of despair. I wanted to quit. I felt like I couldn't win. These moments made it seem like attempting to overcome my injury was a mountain too high to climb.

Upon continuous days of frustration, disarray, and emotional depression, I became fed up with the feeling of defeat. Instead of continuing to feel defeated, I began to focus on specific action steps to help me win. I identified changes that I needed to make in order to change the way I felt. I also identified specific things I could do, such as increase my education, establish a workout regimen, and change my eating habits. I also took a look into the future in order to clearly define what it was I wanted to accomplish in life and to identify all of the necessary steps I needed to take in order to complete those accomplishments. I began to look at the things that I wanted the most. For example, I knew I wanted my own house one day, so I focused on understanding all that it was going to take for me to not only purchase a home, but to make sure the home was accessible for me in the event that I was still constrained to a wheelchair. Despite my disability, I wanted to learn to drive, so I began to learn about hand controls and how much they cost and where I needed to go in order to have them installed. I also wanted to understand the driving regulations for someone with a severe disability, so I researched and studied all the information I could find.

I took the time to figure out and plan everything that I wanted in life. Next, I applied specific steps that I would take in order to make it happen. These were my action items. These were things that I could be doing instead of moping around feeling sorry for myself. This was my planned attack to accomplish what I wanted. I mapped it all out in an outline. I created an environment where I never had a dull moment. There was always something that I could be doing that would help me get where I wanted to go; even if it just meant reading a specific book about a particular topic, studying for tests, or conducting research for open jobs.

Planned action is anything that will pull you closer to your goals. It can be as simple as reading a book in order to gain knowledge about a particular topic of interest that will heighten your awareness of the goal you are trying to reach. For example, part of my planned action was spending the time with my mentor, and practicing activities of daily living in order to become more independent. I also learned how to maneuver my wheelchair in and out of tight spaces quickly and safely, and played around with Lego blocks in an effort to increase the dexterity in my hands. Planned action was anything that would help me take my mind off my current condition and overcome the situation I was experiencing. It was simply doing things every day that brought me closer to achieving my goals.

Planned action helps defeat moments of despair. I personally feel that it is insane to be dissatisfied with a particular area in your life, and then to respond by doing nothing about it. However, after my accident, that was the state I was in—I was emotionally distraught with my current situation, but I wasn't doing anything about it. So I decided to change that and take action and strategic steps forward that would produce a positive change. As a result, I began to have less moments of despair because I was more focused on my goals and success. I didn't spend a lot of time focusing on what I couldn't do because I was too busy working on what I thought was possible. It wasn't easy at first, but one of the things I noticed as a result of taking action was that it actually changed the way I felt whenever I got frustrated, depressed, or defeated by my injury. I learned that negative and positive thoughts couldn't occupy my mind at the same time. By focusing on the positives and reaching towards success, I removed the negativity out of my mind. I was filled with positive thoughts because I was working towards positive goals. Having my own pity party and feeling depressed all the time was only perpetuating those negative thoughts and emotions, therefore making me feel more depressed.

To this day, I still have moments of frustration, discouragement, and even sometimes defeat. We all do; however, when I feel that way, I stop, regroup and then ask myself what I can do to correct the situation causing me to feel bad. When action items come to mind, I immediately get up and get moving to do what needs to be done. What I found is not only do I feel better as a result of the positive emotions gained from working towards my goal, but I also increase my productivity. In a way I'm thankful for the moments of disparity because they allow me to recheck myself and immediately begin to focus on actions I need to take. It's a bit of a mind trick, but it works for me. In fact, it has been working for me for years. I believe it will work for you too.

In order to create a strong understanding of planned action, take some time alone in a quiet place without interruptions. Forget all of the challenges and obstacles or situations you face. Focus with vivid clarity on what you want out of life. Visualize what your life would be like if you could accomplish your deepest desires. How would you live if you could live life on your terms? What would you do? Where would you go? How would you live? What cars would you drive? What kind of house would you live in? Where would you live? Would you own a business, become an investor, write books, or run an Internet company? Who would you help?

Once you have answered these questions, picture yourself living that life, helping those people, visiting that country, living in that house, and driving that car. Feel how good it is to live like that and accomplish all of those things. Get emotional about it: Feel it. As the ideas and strategies begin to come to your mind, make sure to record them on paper. Set a timeframe as to when you would like to begin to experience each of the desires you have identified. List the specific things you will need to do to make it all happen. Carefully record each idea, strategy, routine, action step, and intention on paper. Close your mind tightly to all negativity, disbelief, and discouragement. Guard your plan and only share it with those who believe in you, know what you are capable of, and desire for you to succeed.

My recommendation is for you to find someone who has already done what you desire and is willing to teach you and guide you.

Share your plans with him and have him mentor you and hold you accountable for following through on your planned actions. Once your plans are clearly defined, and approved by your mentor, make a vow to complete all of the action items within your plan. With this said, be aware that we live in an imperfect world where things don't always work out exactly as planned. It is probable that you will face temporary defeat or experience moments when you feel things aren't happening fast enough. When you feel afraid, frustrated, discouraged, or uncertain, do not lose focus; instead, respond by taking persistent action towards your plan. During these moments, do something that will propel you towards your desired outcome.

As I reflect back to the early stages of my injury, sometimes I imagine what my life would be like if I had allowed disparity to defeat me. I would probably still be sitting in an electric wheelchair all-day-everyday, perhaps living with my mom or living in a rest- home. I probably would not have a job, or career. I would not have been able to travel and see the world the way I've seen it. Someone would always have to take care of all my needs because I would be unable to handle them myself. I would not have a positive influence on anyone's life, and I would not be able to give you the key principles that have led to my success. These key principles will also lead to success in your life, if you apply them daily.

When you fall into despair, imagine your life 3 years, 5 years, and 10 years from now if you fail to overcome. Will you have the life you desire? How will you look and feel? Will you be satisfied with yourself? Probably not; instead, you will spend the rest of your life wanting and wishing you had something better. However, the opposite of defeat is victory. What if you use the recommendations from this chapter and defeat moments of despair through planned action?

Now imagine how great your life will be in 3 years, 5 years, and 10 years as a result of overcoming, getting up and winning. You will potentially have a lifestyle beyond what you ever wanted or imagined. You will have free time to travel the world, do all you desire to do, and live life on your terms. You'll probably own nice cars, nice houses, be well respected, and most importantly you'll be in a position where you can give back and significantly help change the lives of others.

Determining your goals is crucial to reaching success. You can waste a lot of time and energy moping around and having your own pity party. Whenever you feel down, the best thing you can do for yourself and your current situation is to immediately take action to change it. However, the key to making this work is knowing what action to take. Hence, completing the above exercise is crucial because it outlines the action necessary for getting where you want to be. This practice provides a roadmap to your success. This practice has helped me countless times throughout the grueling challenge of overcoming my injury. I never thought I would experience the misery and desolation this injury placed upon me. Overcoming this injury was the most daunting task I've had to complete. As I've mentioned earlier, it was not easy.

Upon my quest to recover, if it wasn't for this mindset, and implementing planned action, I would not have made it. It was the ability to refocus all of the negative emotions towards a positive outcome that set the pace for my recovery. It is the most important step of all of the principles I've given to you in this book. I assure you, if you consistently apply this practice in your life, you will meet with success. Get up! Take the time now to visualize your dream life, plan the steps to get you there, and take action!

Chapter 16

Look Beyond
Reality and See
What's Possible

When I was lying in the emergency room of Duke University Medical Center, I did not fuss or complain about anything. I just wanted my tests to come back with good news. I wanted to hear the doctors tell me that everything was going to be ok—that I was going to be back on my feet soon because I had only suffered a minor spinal injury that would heal quickly. I knew there was a possibility that things could be really bad, but I tried my best to remain positive. I cooperated with the doctors in every way possible with the hope that it would all be over soon. But I was afraid of the outcome. I didn't know what to expect. It felt like my life was on the line. I knew there was no cure for spinal cord injuries. I just hoped and prayed that nothing serious was wrong with mine.

The nurses assured me that I was stable enough to go to sleep. They gently reminded me they would periodically be checking in on me. I knew I had a lot more tests to take. I woke up in the middle of the night and was greeted by my mother and father. They had numerous questions about the tubes in my mouth, as well as why I had spent hours on a bed that had me rotated to one side. I was very hungry and thirsty when I awoke, but the medical staff would not allow me to eat. I was told that I would be getting an MRI soon so the doctors could decide what to do with my spine. There was still no movement or sensation below my neck.

Because the injury was so fresh the doctors could not offer any type of prognosis as to the severity or the probability of recovery. It was difficult for my family to simply wait. However, my medical team did indicate I definitely suffered a spinal cord injury, and that the MRI would help everyone understand the damage. Based on the level of function and sensation that I had, it appeared that it was very severe; one from which most individuals never would recover. In most cases like mine, the spinal cord swells and causes further damage. As a result, the doctors decided to hold off on the surgery until further tests were completed.

Not long after talking to the doctors, a team came to take me to the x-ray and MRI section of the hospital. At this point I was scared. I didn't know what my future was going to look like. I was afraid for my life. All types of thoughts were going through my mind. I kept trying to move my body on the way to the MRI room. I tried to move my legs and my arms, hoping that there would be some sign of improvement, but nothing happened. I kept hoping and praying that my sensation would return, but it didn't. Once I reached the radiology department, I was transferred onto the MRI platform. It felt tight and claustrophobic inside the scanner. I could hear the voice of the young woman speaking to me from within the speaker system. She wanted to make sure that I was properly positioned and comfortable inside the scanner before she began. I responded back to her with a faint, "Yes, I am okay." As she was taking pictures of my spine, tears began to roll down my face as the devastation, sadness, and fear of the injury hit home. I wanted to get out of the MRI scanner. I wanted to get out of the hospital altogether. I wanted to run away.

Not only was my body hurt and injured, but so were my mind, my emotions, and my entire being. All I felt was pain. Excruciating pain. It was unlike anything I had ever experienced or imagined. Words cannot express how painful this experience was—I cried and cried and cried and cried. I cried so long and so hard that I could not cry anymore. I wanted it to go away.

The only thing that I could do was pray, so I began to talk to God. I began to pray for healing. I asked God to take it all away and remove the pain. I prayed for emotional and physical strength to make it through the rest of the night. I felt like all was over for me. I remember lying there with my eyes closed, talking to God, and praying for a better situation. Hoping for an immediate positive outcome. Before long, I was sleep again. I had literally cried myself to sleep.

Upon waking the next morning, I was greeted by the emergency room nurse who was there to drain my bladder. She explained that I needed to be catheterized every four hours in order to drain my bladder and prevent bacteria from growing. This process made me feel so violated. It made me feel like I wanted to die. One moment I was a young guy with his whole life in front of him, and the next moment someone was pushing a tube into my bladder. I hated every minute of the procedure, and I dreaded knowing that it would happen over and over again. Although they tried to remain strong for me, the look on my mom and dad's faces told me that they were just as devastated.

Shortly after the procedure was done the doctors came through to perform their rounds on all of the patients. My family and I began to immediately question the results of the MRI from the night before, as well as the catherizing procedure. The doctor had nothing to report regarding the results of the MRI. He stated that they were not completed yet and he had not received them. He proceeded to explain the importance of me being catheterized every four hours in order to drain the bladder. He further explained that not only were my arms and legs paralyzed, but my kidneys and bladder were also paralyzed, which prevented me from draining my bladder on my own. Failure to remove the urine from my bladder would cause bacteria to grow, and then infection. An overextended or infectious bladder could cause a sudden rise in blood pressure creating a potentially life-threatening condition called Autonomic Dysreflexia. He stated that Autonomic Dysreflexia occurs most often in spinal cord-injured individuals with spinal lesions above the T6 spinal cord level, and he wanted to take the greatest precaution to prevent such a life-threatening situation, as we did not yet know the severity of my injury. I was devastated beyond any means. Sadness and emotional distress consumed me, and I felt as though I was doomed. I eagerly awaited some type of positive outcome, and began to question when I would receive the results of the MRI.

The next day the doctor came to perform more tests. To my surprise I noticed that I had sensation in my shoulders and partially in my chest. I could shrug my shoulders a little bit, but I still could not raise my arms at all. I was elated to know that there was some return, but was still worried and dissatisfied by the fact that I could not feel or move the majority of my body from the neck down. Upon further tests, coupled with the results of the MRI, the doctors reached the determination that I had suffered a low cervical C5/C6 spinal cord injury. X-ray images concluded I had no broken bones within my spinal column, however according to the MRI scan, it appeared that I had severely bruised my spinal cord as a result of the impact of the tackle. The hopeful news about a bruise, or a contusion, was that the doctors could not determine whether or not the bruise would heal. They did know there was bad nerve damage and some of the nerves would never heal themselves, therefore causing permanent paralysis. This meant there was a slight chance of recovery.

I remember one particular doctor stating that my family and I should prepare for me to be in a wheelchair for the rest of my life. He stated that I would never walk again as a result of my injury, even though it was an incomplete spinal injury. The reason why the doctors called it an incomplete spinal injury was because my spinal cord was not completely severed. In the majority of spinal cord injuries, the spinal cord is completely severed, making the possibility for recovery nearly impossible. During these cases, spinal surgery is performed as the only option for potential recovery. However, in my case the doctors decided not to perform surgery because it was unknown how severe the contusion was, and whether or not it would heal itself. Although not the news I wanted to hear, this provided hope in my mind. I hedged my recovery on the idea of my injury being only a bruise.

I became increasingly optimistic about the idea that if I only suffered an incomplete injury, there could be a high level of recovery. However, the doctors didn't see it that way. Although they had not seen many cases similar to mine in regards to a bruise or contusion, they remained adamant that the possibility of recovery was slim to none. The only expectation the doctors had for my recovery was based on the location of the damage to my spinal cord. The MRI scan demonstrated injury to my spinal cord at the C5/C6 level, which technically results in the potential loss of function in the biceps and shoulders, limited wrist control, and complete loss of function of the hands and all the other movement and function of the extremities throughout the remainder of the body. In other words, I was paralyzed from the chest down.

Over the course of the next couple of days, the doctors continuously performed the ASIA exam. They pin-nicked and probed my body just as the doctors did in the emergency room of South Eastern Regional Medical Center. But this time the doctors were looking for any type of improvement compared to the results of the past ASIA exam. What we found was a slight improvement in the level of sensation in my arms down to my wrist and hands. There was also stronger sensation from my neck to midway down my chest. Below these areas there was no increased movement or sensation. This was now my reality, or what appeared to be my reality.

Looking beyond this, I came to the understanding that we all have the powerful and inherent ability to think whatever we want to think. However, it requires much more effort to think what we want to think than it does to think those thoughts that are naturally summoned as a result of our external environments or appearances.

My environment portrayed an appearance of doom and inability. Darkness filled my view of the present and future image of my life. I had no guiding light. At this point I could not see or imagine happiness anywhere in my life as a result of what I was experiencing. The appearance of my external world was producing corresponding thoughts in the mind that said life was over for me. I had no idea how I was going to recover. I was used to changing and building my body at will by working out and staying active. Up to this point, I had spent countless hours in the gym preparing my body for football. I was fit and athletically built. I was in control of my body and I knew how to keep myself in good shape. Now I was paralyzed without any functional movement. There was nothing I could physically do to help myself and the doctors had done all they could do. There was no place or person I could turn to that could change the situation. The reality of my experience was consuming me, and the only place I could turn was within myself.

The inability to move allotted plenty of time for self- reflection and over the course of time I began to discover my spirituality. This was one of the greatest things that could have happened to me. As I continuously prayed, read, and searched for an answer to the trauma I was experiencing, I discovered what I needed in order to look beyond my current condition into a sea of possibilities. I came to the clear understanding that I am an intelligent, spiritual being created by creative energy, or God. I accepted the notion that I am created in the same image as my creator and I possess the same characteristics. I anchored my faith to the idea that I am able to function the same way this energy functions, thus I possess the ability to create, and the fact that the energy that created me lives inside of me and has the desire to bring increase to my life.

As a result, I decided that despite my injury I was going to create the best, most fulfilling and rewarding life for myself that I could. I vowed to look beyond the current appearances of doom and inability. Instead I developed the faith and belief that all things are possible in my life. I placed my focus and attention on the possibilities of walking again, living a tremendously healthy, wealthy, happy life, and being a blessing and inspiration to millions of people around the world and helping them change their lives.

The debilitating and destructive forces of nature that cause limitations within their present conditions shackle most people. As a result, they focus all of their mental energy on their current limitations, unknowingly creating more of the same. They allow their minds and attention to be immersed and occupied by the distractions of their environment, which robs them of their own vision and focus. They allow the presence of the external to control their thoughts, emotions, and outlook on life. If this is you, you should try to come into a calmness of mind and regain control of what you give your attention and focus.

Your reality is what you choose to accept as your reality. Understandably, there may be an external appearance that shapes what you view as your reality, however, it doesn't have to be accepted as your reality at all. Realizing who you are and harnessing the creative energy that lives within you, gives you an advantage over your external environment and its appearances. You can choose what you think about and focus on, and make your positive internal environment a reality. By embracing and channeling your creative energy, both internally and externally, you can begin to understand the unlimited possibilities for your life.

For inspiration, remember those who have come before us who looked beyond their reality into the realm of possibility. Those who created airplanes, skyscrapers, mini-computers, and cells phones; these were people with open minds who were not afraid of new ideas. Instead of focusing on a limited reality, these people focused on what was possible and followed their dreams. Many people believe they are "doomed" to live in poverty, and endure failure and misfortune because of incomprehensible and uncontrollable forces within their environment. Due to this continuous negative and limiting belief, they repeatedly create their own misfortunes. They focus all of their energy towards this belief, thus creating a physical environment for themselves filled with its remnants.

One must understand that the mind will adopt the character of the impressions that dominate it. In other words, a mind consistently influenced by negativity will develop a negative state of mind. Looking beyond your reality and seeing what's possible requires you to nurture positive forces in your mind and eliminate negative ones. This creates favorable conditions for the state of mind known as faith. Faith means believing beyond your reality. Faith is imagining what's possible and acting upon it. Faith, which is the beginning of possibilities and the foundation of miracles, is the remedy to temporary defeat and overcoming your reality. By having faith in yourself and the infinite one, all things are truly possible.

Your reality has the potential to limit you, if and only if you allow it to control you. If you give all your focus and attention to your external environment and its appearance, you make yourself vulnerable to the paralysis of your current situation. However, by looking beyond the appearances of your external environment into the realm of possibilities, you can discover new appearances, ideas, concepts, and ultimately new realities that propel you to a greater satisfaction of life.

Chapter 17

GIVE GRATITUDE FOR YOUR STRENGTHS WHILE WORKING ON YOUR WEAKNESSES

Giving gratitude for your strengths while working on your weaknesses means being thankful for the strong areas and good things in your life, while continuing to work on those areas that are not so strong and need attention. Often times, we find ourselves so upset or frustrated with our shortcomings and misfortunes that we beat ourselves up and focus on our weaknesses as if they're the worst thing that could happen to us.

However, a change in our paradigm would allow us to become grateful and give thanks for everything, good and bad. We must realize that things could always be worse. Likewise, we need to understand that with the intent to strengthen and develop our weaknesses, things can and will eventually get better. The goal should be to maintain an effective balance between the good things and the bad things, the pros and cons of life.

In my opinion, even when it seems as though everything around us is falling down, there's so much for which to be thankful. Sometimes we take life itself for granted because things don't go our way. It may even seem like life is not worth living. However, life is the most precious thing on earth and we should give gratitude for it on a daily basis. There is always someone in a worse condition than you and often times we make things out to be worse than what they really are. Sometimes we need to slow down, sit back, take a look at things and realize they really aren't that bad after all; or, maybe not as bad as we are making them out to be.

Gratitude helps in this process. In order to receive more, you must be thankful for what you already have. As a matter of fact, what you have should be an indication that you can achieve and receive more. Be thankful for what you have and the ability you used to get it. Having gratitude shows that you have appreciation for where you currently are, even if you desire to do more. Some people are so ungrateful and are never satisfied. Having this kind of attitude makes it difficult to accomplish anything. With this type of thinking, you will always feel that you don't have enough. With that being said, it's okay to desire more and work hard for things; I condone that type of behavior. You should try to desire more and do all you can to obtain more; however, you must also be grateful for what you currently have. Gratitude is not difficult because there are a myriad of things for which we should be grateful. Every single day is a blessing worth giving thanks.

At one time, I was ungrateful for all that had occurred in my life as a result of my injury. I thought it was unfair and that there was nothing good that could come of it. However, I now see things differently. I am grateful for all that has occurred in my life, even my traumatic accident, because several good things have occurred in my life as a result of it. It is the positive things I choose to focus on, while completely ignoring any negativity. It allows for me to live a fuller, happier, and emotionally stable life filled with joy and laughter.

One of the things I give significant gratitude for is my mind. I am blessed to want to do more and have the ability to take action. There are so many people that want to do more, but they just can't make the shift in their mind to do so. They don't know where to start, and they don't know what to do. I'm grateful for guidance, for opportunity, and for understanding. Out of all the things that I've been able to overcome, I still do not consider myself to have reached all of my goals. However, I'm grateful for where I am today. I desire to be able to run and be more independent, but I'm grateful I can walk, even with canes, and that I no longer have to use a wheelchair. I'm also grateful for the opportunity to inspire and motivate so many people. I am grateful for having turned this experience, which initially seemed negative and debilitating, into something that is positive and inspiring. I'm grateful for my family and all those who have supported me along my journey. I am also grateful for the determination that I possess to continue to push through adversity. Most importantly, I'm grateful for faith: continuous faith, strong faith.

Yes, I could find things to bicker and complain about; however, I choose to identify and focus on the positive things. The more I do this, the more joy I find in my life. As a result, when I look around I see that there is more to be grateful for than there is to complain about. I'm sure if you took a close look at your life, you would also find that there's a lot more to be grateful for than there is to complain about. There's no point in complaining because it only produces negative energy that leads to more negative results. However, maintaining a mind of gratitude allows my mind to dwell upon and experience the superior. In addition, gratitude keeps me connected with the infinite one. In the Bible it says, "draw nigh unto God and he will draw nigh unto you." I make it my business to stay connected by way of gratitude.

Every event or circumstance has contributed to the advancement or your current situation. Therefore, I recommend you be grateful for every single aspect of your life. Don't worry about your shortcomings, or the wrongs that have happened to you, or the negative situations you have been involved in: Be grateful. As a result, you will attract the best and will receive the best. When things are going awry, you can adjust your entire mental attitude with a deep feeling of gratitude for all that is good. It is impossible to be in a negative state of mind while having an attitude of gratitude. Being consistently grateful keeps you looking towards what's possible, and prevents you from falling into negative thinking. A person who possesses a grateful mind always expects good things, and from that expectation they develop faith.

A consistent attitude of gratitude produces faith. However, without gratitude, you cannot acknowledge any good, and therefore you will remain mentally and emotionally paralyzed. Having gratitude gives you strength to move forward. By acknowledging the things that you've already accomplished, or the journey that you've already completed, you should be able to possess the necessary faith in order to keep going.

If you have made it this far, what makes you think you can't go further? There's a quote by Thomas Carlyle that says "Go as far as you can see, when you get there you will see how you can go farther." Strengthen those areas that need work. For example, if you are thankful for the fitness level that you have achieved, you should be encouraged enough to continue to move forward and experience greater fitness. In my journey to recovery, I was thankful for every single step that I was able to take, even if it was only one step. As a result of being able to take that step, the next day I could look forward to taking that step again, and maybe even adding a step or two more. We have to be grateful for the small things because they are what help us achieve our larger goals.

Once I became thankful for my life after my accident, I wanted to see what I could do with my life. I wanted to see if I could turn it into something positive and productive. When it comes to working on your weaknesses, you must acknowledge your strengths and be thankful for them by realizing that you could be in a worse situation, stripped of all the strength that you do have. Identify and acknowledge what you have and use it. Be grateful. Utilize all you are grateful for and strive for more. Continue to press forward. If there are any weaknesses that you have identified, be grateful and have faith in knowing that you can work on them until they are strong. This will eliminate the need to complain and bicker about your weaknesses. Focusing energy on the fact that you are weak creates more weakness. Instead, adopt a positive outlook on your strengths and your weaknesses and embrace an attitude of gratitude so that you can live the life you desire.

Chapter 18

ENERGY FLOWS
WHERE FOCUS GOES

Focus has been the heartbeat of overcoming my personal obstacles. It is responsible for moving me in the right direction, and preventing me from falling into depression, addiction, or any of the negative alternatives to dealing with my injury. As a result of my injury, there were a lot of changes in my life that prevented me from doing things that I physically used to do like running, playing football, and being physically active all together, but what also changed was the way my body functioned. There were normal parts of daily living that I couldn't do anymore—things that most of us take for granted. These things tolled the most on my emotions and demanded most of my attention. It was these things that I thought about the most because they hurt the most. I wondered if I would ever be able to overcome them because not doing so would really degrade my quality of life.

I spent a lot of time wishing the pain would go away and the emotional stress would come to an end. Simple things like bladder control and bowel movements were difficult for me. The lack of function in these areas of my life destroyed my manhood. I didn't know how I could go on without regaining control of these simple activities. Day after day after day, I focused on re-learning these things, but it was to no avail. My bodily functions occurred multiple times a day, and someone had to come help me complete these functions around-the-clock. I was devastated. Every time someone had to help me, I felt violated. Most of the time it was my mother or father, or some random nursing aid that was assisting me with these things, and I absolutely hated it. I felt helpless.

One of the darkest and lowest places in my life was when I was expecting a visit from my biological father and his family. My step-father and I were home preparing for their arrival when my system began to feel out of whack and I instantly had a bowel movement that spilled outside of my clothes, into the wheels of my wheelchair, and onto the floor. The only possible way my stepfather could help me get cleaned up was to pull me out of the chair and lay me down on the floor. This was one of several gruesome and horrific experiences, or moments of disparity after my accident. Right at the time this was happening there was a knock at the door, which was my biological father arriving for his visit. Nothing could be done at this time but to proceed with cleaning up the mess, but all I could focus on was the fact that I was lying on the floor and getting cleaned up.

I hated the fact that I couldn't control my own body and that I had to rely on others for help with the simplest things. I hated that this was my life, and that other people had to see me this way. It absolutely consumed my focus, even after everything was all cleaned up and done with. It was all I could think about and in no way, form, or fashion had I rebounded from the emotional trauma I experienced. I felt as though I would never rebound. I felt so low that I began to doubt if my life even had value. How do you rebound from such a traumatic experience? How do you regain your manhood and sense of self-worth? I felt so emasculated that I became anxious about the issue of sex—how was I going to do that in my condition? As a young man approaching adulthood, this was a huge concern for me.

I didn't know how to get the thoughts of defeat out of my mind. I was losing the battle, and I knew it. The only thing that I could do to change my mindset and save myself from the point of no return was to begin to focus on what I could do. At first, this was very difficult because there wasn't much that I could do. It took people like my sister to help me realize that even though I was paralyzed and I was experiencing emotionally debilitating side effects, there were still things that I could accomplish. Unknowingly, she held me to a very important responsibility that changed my outlook and focus on life. Regardless of all that I had to go through and the things that sometimes my sister had to help me with, she still demanded that I play my role and fulfill my responsibility to her as a big brother. She expected nothing less from me. She still wanted to play with me, talk to me, and get feedback from me as a big brother. She still looked to me for protection and all of the other things that a big brother was supposed to provide to his little sister. As a result, I wanted to be the best big brother that I could be. I wanted to be there for her in any way that I could. I wanted to succeed at being her big brother.

I knew I still had a lot going on in my life with which I had to deal, but that did not negate the fact that I had a responsibility to my little sister, and so regardless of what was going on, I had to get over it. I didn't have time to focus on the things I couldn't do because focusing on those things would make me forget about my responsibility as a big brother. So, I did not spend a lot of time focusing on those things, but instead I focused on how I could do what I needed to do—how I could be a big brother. As a matter of fact, I vowed to myself to focus little energy on the things that I could not do, and I set out to do everything that I knew I could achieve. I began to think of things that I wanted to do in my life. I would tell myself that if I ever get the chance to do this, or if I ever get a chance to do that, I'm going to do it better than anybody ever did.

Focusing on what I could do helped me feel better. As you can imagine, focusing on all the things that I couldn't do made me feel awful, worthless, useless, unattractive and selfless. Focusing on what I could do gave me a sense of self-worth and accomplishment, and increased my motivation. It felt so good to be able to accomplish something that I set out to accomplish, and it put my motivation at an all-time high. I found out that there was more that I could do than there was that I couldn't do. When I rank myself up against other able-bodied people, I understand that I can do more than the average person. I understand that I can do all that I set my mind to, as long as my focus is in the right place. Over the years I've learned that energy flows where focus goes.

Focusing on limitations robs you of your precious time. Time spent focusing on limitations could be time spent focusing on your ability to succeed. Unless you're doing something positive to change the current situation, focusing on it doesn't do you any good. It doesn't bring you any value. Therefore, not only is it a waste of time, but it is also a waste of energy. Some people spend all their lives focusing on what they can't do. They never make the switch to focus on their ability to succeed, and as a result, they remain stuck in the same place for their entire lives. All the time and energy spent on worrying and focusing on limitations is of no value because it puts all of your energy in the wrong place. Your energy and focus should be spent on what you can do to improve your ability to succeed. Focusing on what you can't do brings about negative emotions such as stress, worry, low self-esteem, and therefore decreases your quality of life. It plants the seed of negativity, which fosters much bigger problems such as depression and disease. Whereas focusing on your ability to succeed brings about positivity, self-confidence, security, and increases your ability to accomplish your goals. Focusing on your ability to succeed also increases your quality of life and brings about a positive mindset and perspective towards the present and the future.

Often, when my mother and father assisted me with my daily activities, they intentionally talked about things that were unrelated to the current situation. The things we were currently experiencing were negative and we knew it, and it had taken a toll on all of us. Talking about it only perpetuated the situation, so we decided to focus on other things, good things, things that we could do. We often had gatherings and cookouts where we invited family and friends over to have a good time; this helped us enjoy all we could out of life. Of course, there were some things we absolutely needed to talk about. In some cases we were forced to talk and sometimes argue. Nothing was perfect and all things weren't avoidable, but we attempted to focus on how we could make the situation better. We recognized what the limitations were, and we sought to improve them.

I personally made a conscious effort to identify all I could do to improve, and proceeded to focus as much of my energy as possible on achieving those goals. Whenever I found myself focusing too much on what I could not do, I would remember something I could do, and go do it. For example, instead of focusing on the fact that I could not write because of the loss of ability and dexterity in my hands, I would go get on the computer and surf the Internet, or develop a Word document. Likewise, instead of focusing on what I could not do with my friends, I would always inform them of the new gains or small recoveries I experienced, and all the things that I was able to do.

Every time I accomplished one of my goals, big or small, we celebrated. It was a big deal. I specifically remember the first time I was able to wash my face and hair after my accident. Before I got hurt, I was always well groomed and was conscious of my appearance, but that was taken away from me after my injury. I wanted to keep myself groomed the exact way I used to, but I couldn't because I didn't have that ability. As a result of my situation, one thing I learned is that people are not going to take care of you the way that you would take care of yourself. But again, I couldn't focus on what I could not do. I had to accept where I was and focus on making the changes that I wanted to see in my life—and I did just that. So, when I was able to wash my hair and face on my own, you could not get me out of the bathroom! I took pride in this small gain, and I did it to the best of my ability. Every single day, my goal was to make sure my appearance was nothing less than perfect. What I found is that when a simple pleasure is taken away from you and you are fortunate enough to get it back, you no longer take it for granted. I certainly didn't. I am so proud and thankful for everything that I'm able to do now that was once taken away from me early in my recovery.

Stop focusing on your limitations, and start focusing on what you CAN do to achieve your goals. There is no benefit or gain from harping on what you can't do; instead, focus on your abilities, even if they seem small or insignificant. Because that one small thing you can do, will lead to bigger and better things. When you focus on your abilities, you will experience a shift in your mindset from negativity to positivity, and you will see increases in motivation and self-esteem. Don't spend your life stuck in one place, taking things for granted. Look around, appreciate what you have, and be thankful for all that you can do. Energy flows where focus goes, so concentrate on the good, and there will be more and more to be grateful for.

Chapter 19

Even if You Can't Win, Leave it All On the Field

We only have one shot at life, so don't live in mediocrity. Give your life all you've got to give. Don't live a life full of regrets—that you didn't try hard enough, you didn't believe in yourself enough, or you didn't realize your dreams. We can't control everything that happens in our lives, and we may be put in compromising situations; however, it does not mean that you should not do all you can to live the most successful, happiest, fullest and purposeful life possible. If you put forth the effort, you can live the life of your dreams. Instead of focusing on whether you are going to win or lose, focus on how you are going to play the game of life. You want to be able to look back on your life and say you've given it your best; that you did all you could in each and every situation.

Do everything possible to accomplish all you can and live life to the fullest, while leaving something good behind for others. Reach back to help others—show them something positive, so that they can live by the example of your life. When we leave it all on the field, we give the game of life everything we've got and inspire others to do the same. You can't take anything with you when you leave this life. All that we have is only borrowed. It doesn't matter how much money, or wealth, or material things you have because they are meaningless in the end. For this reason, we should enjoy as much as possible while we are here. In addition, we should make it our goal to help as many people as we can during our lifetime.

Despite what life may throw at me, I'm going to press forward and live the fullest and most influential life that I can live. I realize life is going to throw me some curveballs, but I'm going to defeat everything that attempts to stop me from reaching my greatest potential, which is to be the best example that I desire to be and help as many people as I can help. I believe my purpose is to show individuals that anything in life is possible. Sometimes we look at other people's success, and we feel like we can't be as successful. We feel as though there is some type of magical power that has allowed them to be successful while we have to settle for our mediocre lives. Based on what I've been through in my own life, I am here to tell you that it doesn't matter what life you have been given; whatever you desire you can achieve. If you first believe that you can do it and give it everything that you have.

When I decided to leave it all on the field, I was given an ultimatum. I was at a crossroads in my life where I had to decide whether to accept what the doctors told me, or fight to live the life I desired. I made a decision that it didn't matter whether I won or lost, so long as I tried. In the end, what mattered the most was not whether I got out of the wheelchair or not, but rather the steps I took to change the situation. Did I give up and quit, or did I put forth the effort to make a difference? Did I just sit there in my pity and allow defeat to overcome me, or was I going to get up and do something about it? Did I give myself the opportunity for something positive to happen, even if it meant I didn't ever run again or play football again or be 100% the way I used to be? Regardless of the outcome, I still had to put forth the effort to allow some positive change to occur—and that's what mattered in the end.

When I decided to leave it all on the field, I dedicated myself to doing everything possible to get my life back. At the same time, I opened up my heart, mind, and life to others to see me as an example. Hopefully this book is an inspiration that will push you to live your life to the fullest and go hard for what you desire. My hope is that you do whatever is necessary to reach that same level of satisfaction in order to accomplish your dreams. Most of us can't say that. Most of us settle for whatever the doctor says or whatever is considered enough for us to just get by. It is important to realize that we can do more. There's more in us, but many of us choose not to take that route, perhaps because we feel it's too hard or too painful.

Personally, I feel that there's no other way to live my life. Having had everything taken from me at one point in time, and not knowing if I'd ever get it back, I decided to give life my all. I made the effort to go out there and get what I desired despite all the odds against me. I made a decision to go after every dream and every desire that I want in my life, and I'm going to give it my all until I reach my desired outcome. Whatever it takes to learn, whatever is required, whatever networks I need to participate in, whatever businesses I need to create—I am willing to do it all to help however many people I can.

As I mentioned earlier in this book, there was a moment in time when I wanted to give up. I did not want to reach for anything or achieve any goals. All I wanted to do was crawl underneath a rock and die. I didn't have the mindset to press forward, or to put forth the effort to overcome my challenges. I did not have the strength or state of mind to expect any healing or recovery of my body. I was defeated, mentally, emotionally and physically. I contemplated suicide on several occasions. What stopped me from going over the edge was the fact that I knew it was the easy way out. I knew by taking that route I was sure to lose the battle and allow life's circumstances to completely defeat me, consume me, and zero me out of the equation. Even with all my pain, that was absolutely not an option. To take my own life would mean that I had been defeated and beaten to the point of death. Although that was exactly how I felt, I loved myself more than that, and as a result, I made a decision:

I wasn't going to allow my injury to kill me or defeat me. So I had to defeat it, or give it everything that I had to defeat it, in order to be at peace with myself.

You only have one life to live; so it's better to have put forth the effort to accomplish everything you desire than to do nothing at all. One thing is for sure—you can't reach your dreams by doing nothing. If you don't give it your all, you truly can't expect to get all that you desire in return. Therefore, the best possible way of living the most fulfilling, rewarding, and complete life is to give it all you've got. Go after your dreams and your desires with 110% of your effort. Sometimes we have to ask ourselves why we desire things, but are not willing to go after them? We are God's greatest creation—history has shown us that we are capable of doing some of the most miraculous and incredible things. We've done all sorts of things that were once considered impossible. I truly don't believe that there's anything that's absolutely impossible to accomplish.

Many people in this world have gone to great lengths to accomplish great things. Even I have had to go to great lengths to get out of a wheelchair and recover from an injury that doctors said was irreversible. No, I'm not 100% recovered. Yes, I still have to walk with the aid of canes or crutches, but please understand—even that is miraculous and mind blowing! The doctors do not understand how it is possible; however, I know that it is a direct result of me giving it all that I have emotionally, mentally, physically, and spiritually. Nothing is truly impossible for me and I believe that nothing is truly impossible for you. You too can experience all of your dreams. Find out what is required for you to accomplish what you desire and go for it. There's probably someone else out there who's accomplish something similar; establish a relationship with them, find out what they've done, and then go do it yourself. Give it all that you've got.

Don't accept no for an answer. Develop a burning desire in your heart for your goals and do not let it go until it is obtained. Where there is a will, there's definitely a way. Keep pressing and looking for the answer, and somehow, someway a path will be made. Believe in yourself and go the extra mile in order to make it happen. If you believe that it is impossible, then it will be impossible. But if you believe that it is possible, then you open the door for opportunity. You can turn impossibilities into possibilities. You'll be surprised at the number of people who will be willing to help you and show you how to put forth the effort to obtain your goals.

Take some time and reflect on all of the things that have occurred in your life that once seemed impossible. Let that be a reminder that you have what it takes to succeed. Don't let anyone tell you that you have to be super smart in order to be successful and accomplish your dreams. This is completely untrue. Yes, it does require a certain amount of knowledge; however, the knowledge you need can be obtained from a number of different mediums. If you do not have the necessary resources, this does not mean that your dream is impossible, it only means that you are going to have to be resourceful and figure out how you can gather the necessary resources to obtain your goal. It also may require you to be patient. Big things don't happen overnight—they take time, strategic planning and effort. Do not be discouraged by temporary defeat. There's a lot to be gained in every mistake or setback that you encounter, especially since every defeat brings you one step closer to success. Learn from your mistakes, learn from your detours, and apply that knowledge to get closer to your goal.

Last but not least, giving up will surely prevent you from realizing your goal. You must commit. Make up your mind right now that you will never, ever give up. If you quit the race, you can never win. You have to continue until the end, no matter how long it takes, how hard it gets, or what is required. You have to make a commitment to yourself to leave it all on the field until the last whistle has blown, and until there are no seconds left on the clock. You must continue to press, push, fight, and do all that is necessary to get up and realize your dreams!

Chapter 20

COUNT YOUR BLESSINGS, BUT DON'T USE ALL YOUR FINGERS

Blessings. We all have them in our lives. Sometimes they are right in front of our eyes, while other times we have to look carefully to truly identify them. When you lose your ability to walk, you start to think that your blessings are few and far in between. But with a little bit of hindsight and perspective, it is now clear the blessings and opportunity was everywhere. You may feel the same way. Wondering, wishing for the blessings. But I can tell you from first-hand experience that blessings are all around us. I realize that I could have given up very early after my initial injury and not have accomplished the things that I have. But it was the blessings of those around me that supported me throughout my journey and pushed me towards success.

Walking again could have been a meager thought in my mind, never to be realized. However that was not the case. I have defied the odds after my injury. In reflection, I am truly blessed to have escaped the confines of a nursing facility, the constraints of a wheelchair, and to have gained an education broad enough to maintain a comfortable life.

Additionally, I am strong and healthy. There was a time in my life when I couldn't walk or stand. As a matter of fact, I couldn't hold a glass, spoon, or even a fork. I couldn't feed myself. Picking up a napkin to wipe my face seemed like a daunting task. These memories are reminders of where I've come from. They remind me how truly blessed I am today. They keep me rooted in the understanding that nothing in life is guaranteed or promised. Life is an unpredictable journey. However, most significant of all, these memories serve as examples and springboards towards what I could potentially accomplish in the future. I try to count my blessings every day, but I always recognize there are more to come. As I press forward and continue to reach for greater success in life, looking back at what I've already accomplished and the blessings that have come to me provide confidence and assurance in my ability to reach my higher goals.

We should all be thankful for where we are in life. Regardless of present circumstances, things could always be worse. We must be mindful, even in the midst of adversity, challenge, or obstacles, to take a look around and count our blessings. One at a time. Each and every day. Sometimes we focus on all of the things we don't have and those we desire to obtain, all the while forgetting the value in what stands right in front of our eyes. Reaching for success, money, or the finer things in life is great and brings about growth. If properly traveled the journey can bring out the best in each of us.

However, counting your blessings steadies your mind and brings you back into peace and harmony with the present, and all the blessings you received to date. It brings about an attitude of gratitude. It is important to realize what you have before you attempt to reach for more. Remain thankful for where you are in order to receive more. Remember, there's a difference between feeling thankful versus being satisfied.

Once I overcame my nasty attitude and anger that resulted from my injury, I came to the realization that there were many things for which I should be thankful. Although I was paralyzed with the loss of feeling and sensation, or physical movement in the extremities of my body, I was still alive. Not only was I alive, but I had the full use of my mind. I could reason and I could still learn. I had the ability to see, comprehended, and understand. As I watched patients enter and exit the hospital with serious injuries, I began to count the blessing that became more apparent in my life. I still had the gift of thought. I realized that I could be experiencing something much more catastrophic.

One of the most memorable and self-awakening moments was when I was in rehab with a patient who had been hit by car while riding her bicycle. She suffered severe brain damage. Her head was severely crushed on one side. Her skull was so severely shattered that you could actually see that part of her skull was missing. She could not properly function as a result of her brain injury. She wasn't aware of her surroundings. She knew she was alive but she could not reason with the living. She could not comprehend. She could move her body but she could not relate to her environment. That experience and her tragedy quickly gave me some much-needed perspective.

Several years after my accident, I was blessed with the opportunity to attend college and live on campus. My roommate had also suffered a spinal cord injury early in his life. His injury was very similar to mine. Both of our injuries occurred in approximately the same area of the spine. However, he did not have the ability that I had. At that point, I had experienced a considerable amount of recovery and was able to stand and to take a few steps with assistance. Sadly, he was completely bound to his wheelchair. He could not stand at all nor did he have any movement in his extremities.

Through recovering from my injury, I saw several individuals with spinal injuries far worse than the injury I suffered. I've seen some with spinal injuries so severe that they could not even breathe on their own. They had to use a ventilator in order to survive. I've seen others with high-level spinal cord injury that prevented all bodily movement. One of these people communicated by blinking his eyes once for "Yes," and twice for "No." That was all he had left. Witnessing his lifestyle was one of the most difficult experiences for me. Not to mention this injury occurred as a result of having a stroke in his brain stem while playing a summer game of pick-up basketball with friends. Until then, I thought my accident was freaky. This goes to show that you must be very mindful of the things we complain about and the things in life we take for granted. We must be mindful to look around and count our blessings, realizing that in every situation, there's always someone else in a much more challenging and debilitating situation than you.

When it comes to blessings, there must be balance. It is important that you are grateful and consistently count your blessings. However, it isn't a must that you remain satisfied. You can be thankful without being satisfied. Only when you feel satisfied with your environment are you capable of becoming complacent, which is why you should never use all of your fingers when counting your blessings. The remaining fingers should be goals or obstacles you have yet to reach or overcome. I feel it is important that we continuously strive for more, desire for more, and ultimately accomplish more along our journey. We should continuously expand ourselves into new and refined individuals. Reaching for more symbolizes the desire to express yourself in a greater way than you have done in the past.

Even upon experiencing considerable return of my strength and sensation, I still wanted more. I was completely dissatisfied with sitting in a wheelchair. One of my driving forces was my regular trip to the barbershop. For years after my injury, I had to remain in my wheelchair in order to get a haircut. I did not have the strength or ability to get out of my wheelchair and into the barber chair. As simple as it may seem, this really impacted my manhood. At least for me, there was a positive feeling that I got whenever I went to the barbershop, and sat in the barber chair. After my accident, that feeling was taken away from me. I wanted to feel what it was like to sit in the chair again. Whenever I was in rehab, I would actually think of that feeling. It motivated me and stimulated me to push harder, further, and faster in hopes of regaining the ability to sit in that barber chair again. Although I was grateful for the ability I had gained, sitting in the barber chair was still on my bucket list.

The barbershop was not an isolated experience. There were plenty of times where I reached milestones in my life; milestones that impressed my doctors and made my physical therapists proud. In many ways it would've been okay with a lot of people if I never pressed beyond those milestones. In their eyes, I'd accomplished enough. In many cases, I was blessed to have reached these milestones, and in many cases it was unexpected for me to get there in the first place. But I wanted more and at the same time I knew that there was more in store for me. I knew there was more that I could do and more people that I could influence. So I did what anyone would do: I continued to push.

Becoming comfortable with the status quo causes us to become content with where we are in life, and as a result, we don't strive or stretch for more. You either keep moving towards something worthwhile in life, or we are just moving backwards. Becoming complacent causes us to become stagnant and eventually slip backwards in the game of life, rather than continuing to press forward. Reaching for goals beyond our current experiences causes us to utilize the higher faculties of our minds. It causes us to continue on, when everything around us is screaming for us to stop. As a result of moving forward we can discover results and ability beyond expectation.

This is when true growth occurs. The more we develop, the more we have to give to the world. It is our true purpose in life to grow and give. Just as the plants, trees, and all other living things grow and give of themselves to the greater good, we should adopt the same philosophy and vow to grow and develop ourselves in order to abundantly give life to others.

Complacency causes you to shut off the use of your higher faculties and results in the loss of what you've gained. During my recovery, I noticed the amount of weight and muscle I lost. I was a very muscular guy when I was injured, but it didn't take long for all of my hard earned muscle to wither away from lack of usage. The medical doctors called it atrophy and essentially, your muscles can disintegrate from lack of use. Nature has a way of getting rid of what's not being used or fulfilling a purpose.

The same occurs in the game of life. You'll eventually lose what you don't use. In order to continue growing and expanding, we must consistently place demands on our mental and physical selves. We have to welcome growth and invite it in. We become better people and it benefits the entire world. Remember, you are an intelligent, spiritual being and you possess the ability to create. It is your life long purpose. Although challenging at times, the creative process brings out the best in all of us. So don't shy away from experiencing more or become too comfortable with what you have and where you are in life. Continually press on and reach for more. The journey you travel will uncover greatness in you. And that greatness will manifest itself into blessings. These blessings will uplift you, your family, your friends, and all the other people you touch in your life. We all need more blessings, but we should all take the time to pause, take a deep breath, and celebrate all that we have received to this point. The journey of life is one scattered with unbelievable blessings for the taking. We all have them. Just look around you.

Chapter 21

THE PAST IS YOUR EXPERIENCE; THE FUTURE IS YOUR OPPORTUNITY

In order to evolve and grow, it is important to release past circumstances and stop the behavior of using past experiences as a crutch or an excuse for not being able to achieve our dreams. Let go of your past: Stop making excuses! Use what you've learned from your past to capitalize on future opportunities. Up to this point, I have shared a lot of experiences from my past, many of which made me want to give up on life. When I look back at my past, my injury sticks out as the most challenging and unforgiving experience I've had to endure. The type of injury I suffered wasn't fixable and there was no cure. This was something that I had to live with and endure.

Five and six years after the initial injury, I would still look back and ask myself: why? Upon completing college and moving away from home, I would still question my past. However, I came to realize that what is done, is done. We may not like the challenges and obstacles we have had to go through in life, but they serve as lessons (if we allow them to) that prepare us, guide us, and equip us with the necessary tools to move forward in life. Holding onto the past only results in misfortunes, mistakes, failures, and prevents us from progressing on to the next chapter in life. Time continues on—it doesn't hold still for anyone. We must progress from one experience to another with the objective of learning from the past, in order to apply the lessons learned in the present, so we can experience a greater future.

The principles you are learning in this book served me well when I was progressing through life after my injury. I learned and experienced everything included here while dealing with my own challenges. After experiencing such a debilitating and traumatic injury, it seemed as though life had broken me down all the way to the basics. I had hit rock bottom. My focus was on the fundamentals of life—simple tasks like getting out of bed on my own, bathing and dressing myself, preparing meals and feeding myself. These once thoughtless combinations of movements and behaviors were overwhelmingly challenging and nearly downright impossible for me to accomplish. However, upon utilizing the principles I described throughout this book, I worked hard in hopes that I could accomplish these tasks every day.

As challenging and gruesome as they were, I never let go of the idea of independently accomplishing these tasks. Sometimes with tears in my eyes, I pressed on. Sometimes with a sense of worthlessness and lowliness, I continued to attempt to complete them. It was tough, extremely tough. I was frustrated and mentally degraded by the difficulty I encountered when I attempted to complete what should have been such simple tasks. These were random acts of regular, active daily living. Yet, as a result of not having dexterity in my hands and fingers, the ability to complete any of these tasks was downright impossible. I required personal care in order to survive. For a time, I hated the world and everybody in it. However, I had to come to grips with myself and face the facts of my injury: On

August 26, 1993, I suffered a spinal cord injury that left me paralyzed and diagnosed as a quadriplegic. There it was . . . and I had to get over it.

I attempted to go on with life and educate myself via college and graduate school, yet every day that I woke up after the accident, I awoke up with the challenges, stress, and depression attached to quadriplegia. As you can imagine, for years I resented what happened to me on that day. My life changed the moment I attempted to make that tackle on the field. The future was so uncertain that my family and I could only focus on one moment at a time. I was forever changed. However, I had to love myself. Despite all I had to go through and deal with as a result of my injury, I had to maintain self-love and self-worth. Questioning why the accident happened, and holding on to the past, was actually hindering me from moving on with life. Yes, there were major obstacles in front of me, some of which seemed insurmountable, but life moves on as it should. Holding onto the past as an excuse to have pity, or as a reason to settle for mediocrity was and still is absolutely unacceptable. It only kept me from stretching and reaching for what I wanted out of life.

So there came an important time when I had to accept what happened to me. Although I was determined to fight back and recover as much as I could, I had not yet reached the point of accepting what occurred. As such, it wasn't until I was out of undergrad school and living on my own in Maryland that I reached this point of maturity. I remember sitting at the kitchen table of my apartment in Maryland and experiencing a moment of truth and spirituality. It was as if I came to a realization without any mental or emotional rejection of my identity. Before this moment, I never fully accepted that I was the person who suffered a spinal cord injury. I was always fighting back, rejecting the accident as if it never occurred, when in fact it did. I had suffered a spinal cord injury, and as a result, I had a disability and I had to accept it.

Up to this point, I had failed to deal with the past. I had failed to deal with my emotions and mental perspective of my injury. In certain ways, I did feel sorry for myself, although I did not let anyone know it. Often times, I felt like I was not good enough because of my disability. I would blame my accident as the cause of my disability. First I was injured and then labeled a quadriplegic, which meant I was also labeled as handicapped. I took the labeling to heart. It was hard because every time I looked in the mirror, I was reminded of my disability, which reverted me back to the past and my accident. As T. D. Jakes explained in one of his sermons, "I was a public success, but a private failure." And the reason why I felt that way was because my parents, my family, and my friends were very proud of me for graduating high school, going to college and getting a bachelors degree, moving out on my own, and landing a job. It was a BIG deal to have accomplished that in my condition. Determined to reach my goals despite my condition, I was able to accomplish those things by hiring a nursing aid to assist me as necessary, but mentally and emotionally my accident was still defeating me. I was not winning the challenge that I was facing. It appeared that I was winning because of the things I was able to accomplish physically, but emotionally and mentally I was barely getting a punch in. My accident didn't make me less of a person, yet I was mentally and emotionally allowing it to limit me.

What I mean is that it made me feel worthless, but that was just a symptom of the accident. Therefore, I had to develop the mental toughness to gain a perspective and understanding of the symptoms in order to not allow them to affect me mentally and emotionally. If I didn't, I would continually believe that I was worthless. I had already allowed that to happen for several years after my accident. I was imprisoned mentally and emotionally as result of my injury. However, that day when I was sitting at my kitchen table, I let it all go. I let go of the labels. I let go of the notions that accompanied all of the symptoms and side effects one must encounter when dealing with a disability.

Ultimately, it didn't matter whether I had suffered a spinal cord injury or not. Although it adds variables to the equation, it does not change the game of life. For in the game of life, you are either progressing forward or moving backwards. The laws of life do not change and adjust for individual experiences. As a matter of fact, we all have our own challenges and obstacles that we have had to overcome. Some are just more severe than others. However, if we intend to succeed, we must gather up our strength. We must let go of the past and all the gravity and heaviness that comes with it, and instead hold onto the lessons, the good times, the smiles, and the information gained as a result of living that experience. Doing this will allow us to be better prepared and better equipped to overcome our next assignment.

Life is all about experiences. They are nothing more than situations that have had either a negative or positive affect on your life, or shall I say your perspective of life. I hope all of your experiences in the past have been great experiences. If they have not been, it's okay, as long as you move forward. What's most important is what you are able to learn from your past experiences. Allowing a past experience to consume you only holds you down and keeps you from looking up towards opportunity.

I was held down by my accident and I allowed myself to be labeled, but now I realize that it doesn't matter that I suffered this accident; it really, truly doesn't. It really doesn't matter that I have a disability. What matters is what I want and expect and desire from life. What matters now is how I am going to utilize my experience in order to be successful in the future. Am I going to allow the past to defeat me? Am I going to use my past as a crutch or an excuse not to be successful in the future? No. Instead, I realize that I have suffered a challenging experience and made it through, and as a result I'm a stronger, smarter and better-equipped individual for the future.

Having overcome such a traumatic event, I feel like I can handle anything that comes my way. My mind and emotions have been challenged to a point far beyond what I imagined I could over-come, but I did it. And as a result, I look for challenges and opportunities to exercise my mind. That nugget alone has allowed me to take advantage of opportunities that would have otherwise been impossible. My message is simple: let go of the past. Let go of any negative, degrading, or debilitating consciousness of the past. The past is the past and there's nothing you can do to change it. If you're looking for opportunities to have greater and more positive experiences, understand that it doesn't matter what happened to you in the past. Greater opportunity awaits you.

However, if you're busy focusing and handling issues of the past, you will be blinded and unable to see the opportunities of your future. The past is your experience, the present is your experiment, and the future is your expectation. Use your experiences and experiments to get up and achieve your expectations.

Chapter 22

Get Up: The Ground is for the Grass

God's gift to us all is talent and ability. In fact, I believe the amount we are given during our lifetime is more than we could possibly use. Unfortunately for some of us, facing challenges and obstacles in life are the only times that we truly discover the talent and ability we possess. Often times, it takes us looking deep within ourselves to uncover the hidden abilities we have.

But one thing is for sure, we can return our gifts back to God by uncovering, cultivating, and maximizing our talents and ability to reach our greatest potential. Through life, we will likely experience challenges and obstacles that will call into question our grit and resilience. No one is exempt from the hard times or difficulties of life. We all face them. I sure did.

However, what I've learned is that it doesn't matter whether or not you get hit with the challenges or obstacles within life. The reality is you can count on facing a considerable amount of difficulty accomplishing your hopes and dreams. Rightfully so. If it all was easy to obtain, everyone would do it. So let's just face it. You're going to face some type of adversity in your life. Maybe you already have and yours may be greater than those around you. Perhaps the blow you received knocked you off your feet. Literally, that's exactly what happened to me.

However, the true defining moment is whether or not you remain down on the canvas or eventually decide to get back up and fight. During a period of defeat, difficulty, or challenge, there will be multiple decisions you'll be responsible for making. These decisions will either cause you to remain out for the count or give you the will to get back up, and get on with life and win. Challenges come and go, but your ability to respond remains a constant. At times these obstacles may seem insurmountable. Nowadays I don't allow the size of the obstacle to intimidate me. Nowadays, it only means that I will find greater inner strength and discover new ways within to simply overcome. Step up to the plate when life calls your number. It is not your place to remain down whenever life hits you with challenges or obstacles. You are capable of overcoming and achieving absolutely anything and everything that comes your way.

When I was on the ground, determination, faith, prayer, and a will to win all provided the strength I needed to get back up. To this day, my father reminds me that I have a drive that just will not quit. I love the idea of overcoming challenges. It motivates and stimulates me. I became infatuated with the idea of walking again, especially given the odds. I knew that if I could make it happen, it would be a big deal and a great inspiration to a lot of people. That idea alone motivated me to do whatever was absolutely necessary in order to reach my goal.

In addition, there was a life in which I envisioned for myself that didn't include a wheelchair. There were many things that I desired to do in my life that would have been prohibited as a result of a wheelchair and I was not willing to just sit back and allow that to happen to me without first putting forth the effort in an attempt to prevent it. Whenever I thought about life, family, and creating an environment of happiness and peace, my vision was distorted by the disruptions, divergences, and patterns invoked by the need of a wheelchair or the presence of my disability. Today, not all of the disruptions have completely disappeared, but my quality of life is so much better. As I look back at all of the effort required to get to this point, I can truly say that it was worth it. Ever since my accident occurred I've held a vision of what I want my life to be and I've dedicated myself to that vision, unwilling to accept excuses, only results. I've committed to myself to accomplishing all that I can, regardless of my disability or the fact that I've had to use a wheelchair. My philosophy has been and will always be: no excuses.

I attempted to escape the constraints of my wheelchair for over 18 years. Every year, and multiple times a year, I would pay my doctors a visit in hopes of discovering something that could help increase my recovery. Upon every visit I came up empty. They all would encourage me to continue rehabilitation and learn how to live with the injury. With nowhere else to turn, I would do just that. I would work hard as hell in rehab and then come home and work some more. Once I started experiencing new gains and functionality, I would eagerly return to my doctors and show them the improvements. Still there was nothing they could do.

The fact that there was no cure for my condition instilled a sense of self-reliance that I now apply to all situations in life. Especially those of great challenge. As a result, I have developed a great appreciation for self-development and self-help. The things that I have learned about myself along my journey have been tremendous and brought about an awareness that was unknown to me. It is by this awareness that I was able to get up from my previous condition, and it is by the same awareness that I strive and reach for more.

That inner burn led me to The National Rehabilitation Hospital in Washington D. C. for a routine visit. While there, I asked my doctor if there was anything he could do to improve my condition and even allow me to walk again. At the time I was experiencing increased muscle tightness and muscle spasms from my spinal cord injury. Upon review and evaluation of my physical ability, the Doctor and I pondered what would happen if we were able to decrease the muscle tightness and my muscle spasms. His physical evaluation provided evidence that I had strength and ability. The idea was that a decrease in muscle tightness and spasms would allow my arms and legs to move more freely, whereby allowing me to walk more functionally and perhaps without assistance. The Doctors introduced me to what is known as the Intrathecal Pump, a method of dispensing medication directly into the spinal column in order to efficiently reduce spasticity, decrease muscle tightness, and reduce muscle spasms in order to allow my body to move the way I wanted it to. I began the procedure and I was walking and completely gave up the use of a wheelchair not long afterwards.

I just wasn't willing to take no for an answer. When tragedy strikes, how you respond will often define how tragic the end result may be. But you first have to get up. I always tell people: "When you find yourself in a difficult situation, don't panic." Often times, we freak out when we are challenged. We think the world is coming to an end. Stay calm and bring your mind to a state of clarity. Remember that it is not our external world that controls us, but it is our internal world that guides us.

Upon evaluating the situation, determine how we are going to view the issue. What is going to be our perspective on the situation? Nowadays, whenever life throws me a blow, I realize that it is my time to shine. It is my opportunity to showcase my talents and ability. My name has been called, and it's time for me to perform. Lying down and refusing to get up symbolizes defeat and prevents the opportunity for growth. Get up! And get on with life. It's not going to last forever. Sure, it may cause some discomfort and it may even cause some pain. I look forward to the obstacles and hurdles because I desire to be strong. It is like pumping iron or working out. It is the insurmountable amount of force and restriction against my muscles that causes growth. The same applies to the game of life. Those challenges, obstacles, hurdles and difficulties in life will develop, cultivate, and increase your talents and abilities, thereby allowing you to give more of your gift back to God.

It is as if it was designed that way. Lying on the grass causes your inner mental and emotional muscles to atrophy. No one benefits from you lying there and it doesn't help your current situation. At the very least, getting up provides the opportunity for positive change in your situation. More often than not, we would rather avoid the transformation that occurs whenever growth happens. It seems very uncomfortable and at times, it is. Most of us like things just the way they are. We would rather remain at status quo. My transformation was very uncomfortable and painful. Although it appeared my greatest battle was physical, the majority of my battle occurred within my mind. Overcoming the emotional pain and mental degradation of my spinal cord injury, all while attempting to recover my body physically and get on with my teenage years of life, was absolutely the most difficult thing that I've ever done. However, through it all, I was redefined. I've conquered this mountain in my life and, and as a result, I look forward to the benefits that accompany the journey towards greatness.

You too will be redefined every time you make the decision to get up from where you are and get going along your journey towards greatness. There's more to you than you realize. I challenge you to get up and showcase who you really are and to express your ability hidden within. The world is eagerly awaiting your creativity. We all want to see what you can do. Start where you are, and began immediately traveling your road towards greatness. There is much that awaits you.

Throughout this book, I have worked hard to provide you with a great set of tools and principles for you to use along the way. These principles have been my guiding light. They provided a shining light whenever my world was filled with darkness. Not only that, they have allowed me to get up from where I was and get going toward where I wanted to go.

And in many cases, I can say that I have arrived. I've been able to accomplish some things that I never imagined that I would, especially after my injury. But now I have become aware that I am capable of accomplishing so much more. I hope the words and ideas, concepts and philosophies that I have passed on to you will be your guiding light and your bridge to greatness.

Although we have reached the end of this book, there are plenty of chapters yet to be written within our own books. Take the words of this book to heart. Allow them to rest with you always, and revisit them daily. Let them be an inspiration to you at the time of trouble, and motivation to you in the time of temporary defeat. Let my life be an example that anything is truly possible for those that believe. You can accomplish all that you set your mind out to accomplish. There is no excuse not to. If I can do it then so can you. There was a time when I thought that I couldn't do it. There was a time that I did not believe in myself. I packaged up all of the things that allowed me to believe in me and came to the decision that I was going to do it. I strengthened and developed my will, and eventually my dream came true. You now have the know-how to do the same. Make the decision today to get up and get on with life and turn your dream into your reality . . . and when all else fails, remember:

GET UP!

YOU CAN . . . AND YOU WILL . . . TRUST ME . . . I DID.

BIBLIOGRAPHY

Burrows, S. (2012). About Scott Burrows Motivational Speaker. Retrieved from Scott Burrows Vision Mindset Grit: http://scottburrows. Com/ scotts-story/

Cromartie Temple of Praise . (2007, April 30). Retrieved from Cromartie Temple of Praise : http://www. Netministries. Org

Hawking, S. (Unknown). Stephen Hawking - Home. Retrieved from Stephen Hawking: http://www. Hawking. Org. Uk/

Helen Steiner Rice Poems: Inspirational and Friendship Poems. (2014, December 28). Retrieved from Reconnecting Mind Body Spirit: http:// www. Areconnecting. Com/helen-steiner-rice. Html

Hill, N. (2009). Think and Grow Rich. In N. Hill, Think and Grow Rich (p. 229). Chichester: Capstone Publishing.

Holliwell, R. D. (2004). Working with the Law. In R. D. Holliwell, Working with the Law. Camarillo: DeVorss & Company.

Napolean Hill Quotes. (n. D.). . (2014, December 27). Retrieved from Quotes. Net: http://www. Quotes. Net/quote/14193

Napoleon Hill. (2014, December 27). Retrieved from SelfGrowth. Net: http://www. Selfgrowth. Com/experts/napoleon_hill. Html

PARÉ, M. (2014). Bio Artist Inspirational Story: MARIAM PARÉ. Retrieved from MARIAM PARÉ: http://www. Mariampare. Com

Proverbs 23:7. (n. D.). In King James Version (KJV).

Robins, T. (2010, May 25). Christian Arts Connection... Book Review: Walking Miracle by Art Sanborn. Retrieved from Christian Arts Connection: http://christianperformers. Blogspot. Com/2010/05/book-review-walking-miracle-by-art. Html

Wikipedia. (2014, December 10). Teddy Pendergrass Wikipedia. Retrieved from Wikipedia: http://en. Wikipedia. Org/wiki/ Teddy_Pendergrass

ABOUT THE AUTHOR

Rodney Flowers is author of the life-affirming and highly-inspiring book, Get Up!, I Can't, I Will, I Did . . . Here's How! He is also a co-author of the Amazon bestseller, Unwavering Strength, Volume 2, which is a moving collection of stories by 35 gifted authors. Each story demonstrates that while adversities may be inevitable, overcoming them always leads to the same outcome: growth, healing, and transformation.

In addition to his writing, Rodney has gained a well-earned reputation as a vibrant role model who has a tremendous impact on every life he touches. Rodney's joy for life is infectious. This is exemplified by his sincere, heartfelt passion for motivating, transforming and encouraging others to embrace and live their life purpose to the fullest.

After a traumatic high-school football injury in 1993, Rodney was bound to the confines of his wheelchair. Although he was told his prognosis for recovery was unlikely, Rodney knew he would turn things around, make an impact on the world, and walk again.

With self-determination and a faith in his ability to persevere, Rodney graduated from St. Andrews Presbyterian College with a Bachelors of Arts Degree in Business Administration. To further his education he earned a Professional Masters in Business Administration from the Florida Institute of Technology.

Today, Rodney has contributed more than 14 years of his life to governmental service with the Department of Defense (DoD) United States NAVY (USN). He works for NAVAIR at the Patuxent River Naval Air Station as a Contracting Officer. There he leads a team of seven to 10 contract specialists responsible for executing and managing contract performance of all sustainment contracting actions for the P-3C Orion program, and the P-8A program.

As a result of Rodney's quality of service and outstanding support provided as an individual with a disability, he has been featured in the United States Government's, Careers and the Disabled magazine.

Rodney is well-known and respected within his community as a generous entrepreneur who provides rental properties to those in need through his real estate company.

Rodney Flowers resides in Maryland, where he has also created a business that helps people overcome challenges and obstacles, so they can live joyfully with purpose and realize their dreams.

Rodney is an avid reader who enjoys working out and traveling. He also has an unstoppable belief in teaching others how to get everything they can out of life.

To find resources and information that teach important life practices that assure you will always get back up when adversity strikes, visit www. RodneyFlowers. Com.

48384698R10099

Made in the USA
Middletown, DE
17 June 2019